MISSION TO HANOI

OTHER BOOKS BY THE SAME AUTHOR

American Negro Slave Revolts (1943)

Essays in the History of the American Negro (1945)

The Negro People in America: A Critique of Myrdal's 'American Dilemma' (1946)

To Be Free: Studies in Negro History (1948)

A Documentary History of the Negro People in the United States (2 vols., 1951)

Laureates of Imperialism: Big Business Rewrites American History (1954)

History and Reality (1955)

Towards Negro Freedom (1956)

The Truth About Hungary (1957)

The Colonial Era (1959)

The American Revolution (1960)

The World of C. Wright Mills (1961)

Dare We Be Free? (1961)

And Why Not Every Man? (1961)

American Foreign Policy and the Cold War (1962)

Soul of the Republic: The Negro Today (1964)

One Continual Cry: Walker's 'Appeal' (1965)

Nat Turner's Slave Rebellion (1966)

MISSION
TO
HANOI

by HERBERT APTHEKER

With Prefaces by
TOM HAYDEN and STAUGHTON LYND

International Publishers • New York

Contents

Prefaces

by Tom Hayden

Herbert Aptheker's report on Vietnam should be printed in our country's largest news magazines. Instead it may well be a comparatively little read obituary for the Vietnamese people if the war last as long as seven years, as is projected. As these words are written, we may have "tied one arm of the Administration behind its back," as pro-war advocates often say of the peace movement, but it now seems clear that the one free hand is enough to smash the war into Indochina and China itself. How far toward this kind of war we have traveled in the last few months is indicated in this simple fact: We now have more troops in Thailand than we did one year ago in Vietnam, yet almost no Americans see that the location of the war is drastically widening.

Strangely, our Administration agrees with many of the facts that Herbert Aptheker presents. There are ample statements from Senators, generals, intelligence and technical assistance experts, and journalists to prove the point which James Reston reported from Saigon last September 1: "Even Premier Ky told this reporter that the communists were closer to the people's yearnings for social justice and an independent life than his own government." That the Hanoi government and the National Liberation Front are competent, even representative, is not really in doubt despite regular propaganda blasts from

7

Washington to the contrary. It has been said that our government holds to a devil-theory of communism that makes it paranoid and violent. But what if our government has most of the facts, and still is paranoid and violent? What if knowing the facts heightens our government's need to escalate the war? Then what are we who treasure facts to conclude?

Look at it this way: Vietnam has emerged from the wings of history to become the stage for the greatest social drama of the twentieth century. For decades the "great powers," including communist powers, have placed their national interests above those of the Vietnamese, the result being a distortion of the Vietnamese revolution. The "great powers" have been unsuccessful in even ending the struggle in a way satisfactory to themselves; the Geneva Agreements of 1954, for example, merely delayed and irritated the conflict. From those agreements the Vietnamese learned that the West could not be trusted to keep its treaties, and the great communist societies could not be counted on as the main force guaranteeing national independence. "The Soviet Union and China are both our friends and we welcome their assistance," we were told again and again, "but we Vietnamese make the final decisions."

The United States is killing Vietnamese, I think, to serve notice that revolutions upsetting the world power balance will not be tolerated. Against the idea of a revolutionary war with popular support, which they understand the Vietnamese are fighting, the American government sets the idea of the hydrogen bomb. We are determined to show that no human force is greater than our technological power; as Secretary McNamara considerately put it to a House Committee January 25, 1966, the Pentagon today could wreak "an unacceptable degree of destruction on both the Soviet Union and Communist China simultaneously." Only at this point, when the enemy is "rooted

8

out" and "warned," will the United States be ready to go ahead fully with its blueprint for a Great Society in Asia.

The war in Vietnam once was a gash, but now threatens to split the world. The Vietnamese did not ask for it. What they ask is that the citizens of all the Great Societies look at Vietnam as the majority of Vietnamese do, not as various national interests demand. This is why they are so deeply, touchingly moved by the courage of Norman Morrison, the American Quaker who burned himself outside McNamara's windows. Morrison, says a Vietnamese poem, was "a man of this century," one who could act from an identification with the Vietnamese even though he was American and far away.

I think Herbert Aptheker, the human being, was moved deeply by his experience with the Vietnamese. So was Staughton Lynd, and so was I. The times in this book that Herbert goes beyond the facts to give something of the sense of life in that exciting country, are the times when Herbert writes too as a "man of this century." In our own ways, and the ways will be many, all the rest of us must act as men of this century, saying: "Let Vietnam be for the Vietnamese. We do not want to tell them what they should do. We want to learn from what they do, and in learning together move out of the impasse that crushes us all. Our government will do what it will, but our words and deeds will show that we ourselves are not at war with Vietnam."

Newark, New Jersey
March 6, 1966

9

by Staughton Lynd

Tom Hayden speaks for me but I will add a few words.

Our Christmas journey clarified somewhat the negotiating position of the National Liberation Front and the government of North Vietnam, just as we hoped.

Beyond this it represented two things:

1. *Unity on the Left.* We three—aged 50, 36, 26—represented three different experiences of socialist politics in America. Just as we spent hours together around tea tables attempting to understand our Vietnamese friends, so we spent other hours around breakfast and supper tables attempting to understand each other. Nor did we merely talk: *we did this thing together.*

2. *Internationalism.* The most serious danger to the world socialist movement in the twentieth century, I believe, has been, is, and will continue to be not attack from without, but a tendency toward national self-sufficiency within. The behavior of the Second International in. 1914 illustrates this classically but the same spirit has appeared in the Communist parties, too.

Our trip sought to exemplify these words of C. Wright Mills: "We must become internationalists again. For us, today, this means that we, personally, must refuse to fight the Cold War; that we, personally, must attempt to get in touch with our opposite numbers in all countries of the world—above all, those in the Sino-Soviet zone of nations. With them we should make our own separate peace."

New Haven, Conn.
March 13, 1966

10

MISSION TO HANOI

Prologue

I was one of about one hundred Americans who participated in the Peace Congress held in Helsinki in July 1965. While there, a member of the Peace Committee of North Vietnam asked if it would be possible for me to visit his country and investigate first-hand conditions, ideas and prospects there. He added that the Peace Committee would be especially pleased if I found it possible to come as one of a party of three and that the Committee would prefer that my companions be people whose views and politics were different from my own. I said I would try.

Soon after my return to the United States, I sought out Professor Staughton Lynd, whom I had met two or three times before, whose reputation as a fellow-historian was, of course, well known to me, and whose courageous participation in civil rights, civil liberties and peace activities had long gained my great respect. Professor Lynd said he wanted to go and together we asked Mr. Tom Hayden, founding President of the Students for a Democratic Society, if he would join us. He said he would and then it was only a matter of finding the period most suitable for all three of us. That period proved to be the weeks just prior to, during and after Christmas 1965.

We took the long journey then. So much of the "factual" reporting in the U.S. press concerning matters of dissent and challenge is inaccurate that it did not surprise me that even so elementary a thing as our route was everywhere misrepresented—probably because the FBI supplied information about our original routing which, due to plane cancellation, had to be altered. At any rate, we flew from London to Prague to Moscow to Peking and to Hanoi, and returned via Peking, Moscow, Prague, Zurich, Paris, to New York. Our stay in North Vietnam lasted ten full days; we left on the eleventh day. In our visits to Prague, Moscow and Peking—a total of perhaps another ten days—we also visited and had long conversations with leaders of the Democratic Republic of Vietnam and of the National Liberation Front of South Vietnam.

Shortly before we left New York City, we had read President Johnson's statement that he desired his representatives to "knock on any door" in what Mr. Johnson announced as a new and intense peace-seeking campaign. While none of us saw himself as the President's representative, we did feel encouraged that the President announced the positive-seeking for an end to the fighting in Vietnam as his top-priority concern, at that time.

We knew that the possibility of retribution existed and that what we were doing might be viewed as violating certain statutes; this was especially true of the so-called Logan Act, but we knew, too, that such legislation was of highly dubious constitutionality and that the Logan Act itself—though about 170 years old—had never been enforced and that Mr. Logan himself had not been prosecuted!

Further, in Arthur M. Schlesinger, Jr.'s *A Thousand Days: John F. Kennedy in the White House* (Boston, 1965, Houghton Mifflin Co.), issued just as we were leaving, was to be found this highly relevant paragraph (p. 700):

"The Attorney-General [Robert Kennedy] also strongly supported the move [in 1962] within the executive branch to lift restrictions on American travel to China, Albania and other forbidden lands. Within the State Department [Abba] Schwartz, Averell Harriman and George Ball had recommended that restrictions be removed for all countries save Cuba; and the President several times gave instructions that this be done. But the Secretary of State always felt it was the wrong time to do it, whether because a bill was pending in Congress or a negotiation pending in Moscow; and as a result nothing ever happened. The Attorney-General went even further than the internal State Department proposal and favored lifting restrictions on travel to Cuba as well. It seemed to him preposterous to prosecute students who had a desire to see the Castro regime in action: 'Why shouldn't they go?' he once said. 'If I were twenty-one years old, that's what I would like to do this summer.' "

In any case, I expressed my motivation at the time; prior to departing I prepared a written statement which was to be released when our presence in North Vietnam had become a matter of public knowledge, and this statement was then published. It follows:

There may be some interest in the fact that I have decided to visit the Democratic Republic of Vietnam.

I find the Vietnam war to be among the worst activities in the history of the U.S. government; since that government once was the citadel of chattel slavery, this is no minor criticism!

It is clear—it is repeatedly admitted, even in the American press—that the reportage available to American readers may be aptly characterized, to speak with restraint, as exceedingly one-sided. As Secretary-General U Thant said, "With war, the first casualty is truth." This is doubly so with atrocious and utterly unjust war.

The opportunity to visit the country being mercilessly bombed—with no declaration of war—by forces of the United States and to see for myself what has been done and is being done, and to hear for myself the viewpoint or viewpoints from that other side, therefore, is one that I could not forego. Perhaps I shall be of some service, no matter how modest, in removing the layers of falsehood weighing like an albatross about the necks of most Americans. Certainly, I shall try; I shall exercise my right as an American to "go see for myself," and having seen, I plan to tell and write about what I have seen.

My objective is to do whatever I can *to help stop the killing in Vietnam;* each mite helps and no person must refuse to do whatever his conscience bids toward this absolutely indispensable goal.

I am a writer; in Vietnam is the story of stories and I am going to examine it, first-hand, and then I am going to tell that story to as many of my fellow-Americans as I can.

Now before the reader is that story. Part One contains impressions written down fresh during the days spent in North Vietnam. In Part Two is stated the case against the Administration policy, as I see it after the trip and on my return to the United States. In Part Three is gathered documentary material presenting the viewpoint of the DRV and the NLF, including some data until now unavailable in the United States. Finally, there is appended a selected bibliography on the Vietnam war.

Not least among the values of this journey was the companionship it offered with Staughton and Tom. It was not possible to visit the lands we did without learning; and it was not possible to spend hundreds of hours with those men without learning—in many ways a great deal more. We never hid our differences; on the contrary. But at no single moment in those hundreds of hours was there anything but good-will and, I believe, mutual affection. Our differences were not small but our agreements were overwhelming: We despised the war in Vietnam, we hoped that our journey might make some contribution, however small, to stopping the slaughter, and we planned to give of our energies to that sacred purpose.

PART ONE

In North Vietnam

On arrival in Hanoi, Tom Hayden, Staughton Lynd and Herbert Aptheker (left to right, center) are greeted by representatives of the Vietnam Peace Committee.

1. *There Are So Many Children . . .*

It is the Christmas season back home, where responsible statesmen are considering the bombing of this city—of Hanoi. I walk the tree-lined streets; about me are hundreds of people going about their business. There are many little children and and many, many women.

It is absolutely fantastic. A short time ago at home on my TV, a Senator was explaining how necessary it was that we bomb Hanoi.

He thought—it was Sen. John Tower (Republican, Texas) —that not very many civilians would be killed, but that without bombing Hanoi the vital interests of the United States would be threatened.

It was monstrous at home.

But here?

Here it is like a nightmare.

Is it possible that any government—the American government—is seriously considering whether or not to destroy this city, 13,000 miles away from Washington? To blow apart this woman, burn alive this child, tear apart this building?

In Hanoi live one million men, women and children.

Not one has harmed an American, and most have never seen an American. No one here threatens Los Angeles or Detroit or Brooklyn. Everyone here desperately wants to live in peace—finally—after 25 years of war. Yet back home crackpot "realists" insist that the city threatens U.S. interests.

19

In a factory in Hanoi—a former French colonial prison—producing farm implements and auto parts; note weapons at the ready.

And back home these crackpots think that bombs will frighten this people; this people who for 25 years fought the French colonialists and the Japanese fascists and beat them both.

Their entire history is filled—for 2,000 years—with the passionate quest for independence; this they will have or death.

Is not liberty or death an American slogan?

Did not the United States begin with the revolutionary struggle for national independence?

In the Declaration of Independence of the Republic of Vietnam, adopted in September 1945, the very words of our own immortal declaration are quoted.

20

In the middle of Hanoi is a lovely, large lake. Normally, I am told, flowers adorn its borders, but now air-raid shelters have replaced the flowers. The city glows with light; the cinema is crowded; everywhere men and women are armed.

There are so many children. Many have been evacuated, but there are hundreds playing in the streets. They are playing catch, or tag, or running about the air-raid shelters, or in and out of the trenches that abound; grandmothers watch them. The children and the grandmothers are targets. Everything is a target for a Pentagon gone mad; the whole city, and country, and continent, and world.

I have known this before, but now I am standing in the midst of a prime target and all I see are children and grandmothers.

There is not the slightest hint of panic here. Folks back home are more nervous; here there is determination and dedication and earnestness. Where there is no guilt, why should there be fear?

Posters abound: For independence; death to the aggressors; the world's peoples are with us; hail all fighters for peace.

It is morning. The target remains, intact.

I am in a factory; it is in Hanoi. The newly-constructed building stands on the site of a former prison of the French colonialists. Now there are 1,000 men and women working, producing agricultural tools and parts for automobiles. Forty per cent of the machinery they use was made right here in Hanoi; the remainder came from the USSR and Czechoslovakia and France.

They work eight hours a day, six days a week. They work hard and they put themselves into the work. Almost all study evenings, too.

At their sides stand their rifles. Military practice is frequent, and the best marksman in the plant is a young woman.

21

Many women are to be seen at skilled work. Note rifle at the machine.

The author and Tom Hayden are greeted; note cartridge belt.

22

I meet a veteran of the battle of Dien Bien Phu. The plant director explains that he is in charge of the defense of the plant. When the fighting starts, says the director, he will be the director.

The hero of this republic is an American, Norman Morrison, who immolated himself to protest the atrocious war. One of the workers has made a large poster, and it is displayed at an entrance to the factory. It shows a man wrapt in fire and below are the words: "Morrison's flames will never be extinguished."

Everywhere are the air-raid shelters.

The director says: In the past the word, America, meant to us "beautiful," but now. . . .

He talks of the factory and the workers, of their rest home on the coast that now cannot be used.

He shows us the half-finished addition to the plant that has stopped because what can be gotten out must be gotten out at once. The new life is a good one, he says; no longer are we hungry; no longer do we have overlords, and we are determined to keep our independence. Whereupon he weeps without restraint.

Everyone speaks softly here, everyone appears mild and the women are fabulously dainty and lovely. Everyone is armed.

Here is a village about 20 miles south of Hanoi. In it are 880 families with about 4,500 people and again hundreds of children. All able to carry a rifle do so, in the fields and at school.

Before the Liberation, the landlord owned 70 per cent of the land and the people were hungry and in tatters. In 1945 in that village, 137 peasants died of starvation. Now there is no landlord, and instead of 2,000 separate plots of land, there are 95, and no one is hungry.

At a village near Hanoi "fruits of the village"—a gift to honored friends—are presented to Aptheker, Lynd and Hayden.

All are being educated; medical care is free; 75 per cent own a bicycle; 85 per cent of their homes are of brick; in 1965, 500 tons of vegetables were sold in the city.

Life in the village is pleasant; before, in the time of hunger, there were quarrels and fights, but now in the cooperative there is fraternity.

In the past, our village was like a stagnant pool, but now all is in motion.

We have widened our roads, and enlarged our lake, and improved the drainage, and no one will take this from us.

If Johnson carries his war to our village, we will protect it.

Again air-raid shelters abound; atop them children romp.

Almost all the men in the village now are elderly; the others are in the army. The women are tilling, and raising children, and standing guard at home. The elderly men work, too, and they have formed their own defense unit—the villagers call it the grey-haired force.

There has been such hard work here. Every irrigation ditch, every building—"structures" they are called in the U.S. Air-Force reports of successful raids—every bicycle represents so much hard work. How in the name of decency can anyone think of bombing these things? But then where is the decency, if one can bring himself to incinerate children?

One of the women I speak with in Hanoi has been to international gatherings; there she met American women. They are just like me, she says. They love their husbands and their children; they want to see their children grow up. I think, she says, the American women are as sentimental as I am— full of love. Is that not so? Still, she adds, the most marvelous thing is freedom—freedom and independence and these we will never yield.

Hanoi abounds in air-raid shelters, but there are no barri-

Children of the village gather to greet the guests.

The peasants take the guests on a tour of the fields.

caded hotels or restaurants here such as we have seen in pictures from Saigon. There is no danger from within here; the danger is only from without and from above.

The Museum of the Revolution in Hanoi commences with arrows dating back 2,000 years; it was such arrows that the ancestors of the present people hurled against aggressors.

A professor of history is explaining this and other wonders to me as we move along from hall to hall. And then on the wall I see a photo of three men in prison, heroes of the resistance against the French, and in the middle is—my professor and guide.

Yes, he says, there I am some 12 years ago, and I was there over two years, but I escaped with the people's help.

With the people's help, with the people's determination, this nightmare can be ended and children here and at home, here and everywhere, can live. War belongs in museums; peace must inherit the earth.

26

At the request of the village hosts, the author plants a tree.

2. Bless You, Harry!

Here in Hanoi I have heard that Harry (Two-Bomb) Truman has denounced the shamelessness and self-seeking nature of the exploit whereby three Americans have taken it upon themselves to visit the Democratic Republic of Vietnam even though the State Department opposes such visits. The Voice of America says that the three criminals face five years' imprisonment for their awful act.

Speaking only for myself, I do not take lessons in morality from Two-Bomb Truman; of course, when he speaks of self-seeking he should know what he is talking about, but in this instance he has judged others by himself and this has led again to serious error.

If Two-Bomb Harry wants to know what this war is all about he need but recall the name of his home town in Missouri; and is it not the proud boast of folks from Missouri that they've "got to be shown"—that they want to see for themselves?

I am writing this on New Year's Eve; it's a bright and fairly warm day here. Early in the morning I went, quite alone, for a stroll through the city. The lake is lovely and women were busily preparing flower stalls. People noticed the stranger; some smiled and young children called. There was not the slightest trace of hostility—on the contrary, nothing but friendliness.

I came upon a large bookstore and entered. During the plane trip to this city I had read Nina Gourfinkel's splendid book on Gorky; with Two-Bomb's denunciation in mind I recalled a passage from that book where a police report on young Gorky is quoted. The Tsarist dossier began: "He is an extremely suspicious man; he has read a lot. . . ."

The store was crowded with men and women, the men either elderly or soldiers. I could make out some of the authors and Two-Bomb really has something to worry about.

The workers of Hanoi had before them the works of C. Mac (Karl Marx), F. Ang-Ghen (F. Engels), V. Le-Nin, Onore Da Banzac (Balzac), Dic-Kenx (Dickens), Pus-Kin (Push-kin), Giooc-Gio A Ma Do (Jorge Amado), and Gooc-Ki— the same "extremely suspicious man" who had worried the Tsarist cops.

Albert Maltz's novels are to appear here soon.

And that Hanoi is really the center of a world-wide conspiracy threatening U.S. interests is proven by the fact that Two-Bomb's fellow-Missourian, Mark Twain, is beginning to appear in Vietnamese. By the way, I wonder if Harry S. would like to cover a bet as to how Mark Twain would have felt about this Vietnamese war—complete with napalm bombs and beneficent gasses?

A man from the Moscow Bureau of the *Herald-Tribune* called me last night (I hope this does not make him a criminal too?) and asked if I would be visiting the bombed areas and the front. I said I would. He seemed a little surprised and asked, why. It never occurred to me that a reporter would ask such a question, but my answer—judging by his prolonged silence after he heard it—seemed to surprise or puzzle him a little. For of course I said: "I think it will be good for my soul."

Pardon me, Two-Bomb, if I appear personal, but this criminal wonders how your soul is these days? But, then, this is New Year's Eve and let us not think of unpleasant things. On this New Year's Eve, Harry, would you not toast a 1966 that finds the earth peaceful at last? Bless you, Harry—and every one!

Le Duan, First Secretary of Central Committee, Vietnam Workers Party, greets the author.

3. *Independence Is Existence*

Fronting a lake in Hanoi is a cafe—it is called, indeed, "By the Lake" cafe. Before liberation, it was frequented only by the French colonialists and the few rich Vietnamese. Now as I walk through it those present are the working people of Hanoi, sipping coffee or beer, chatting, admiring the view— with guns nearby.

A member of the Vietnam Peace Committee and of the National Assembly of the Republic explains to me that for the people of Vietnam, independence means quite literally existence. He wants me to understand this.

Under the French rule, which lasted 80 years, millions starved to death and countless thousands were executed or massacred. Under the Japanese, tens of thousands more among the best patriots gave their lives. And then when the French returned, with American guns and dollars, another 150,000 lost their lives until the French yielded and withdrew in 1954. Thereafter under Diem, puppet of the United States, another 150,000 of the best were done to death, tortured, shot, beheaded; this up to 1959 when the veritable war being waged by Diem against the people of South Vietnam forced the appearance in 1960 of the National Liberation Front.

The contemporary experience of the Vietnamese therefore —quite apart from a history of 2,000 years' resistance against foreign invaders—demonstrates that existence without independence either is impossible or intolerable. This explains the fierceness with which the entire people fight for an end to foreign intrusion, for independence.

And there is something else. To the peasant, my companion continues—and 90 per cent of us are peasants—independence meant the land was his, and with the land existence became bearable. That is, the movement that brought independence was the movement that solved the land question for the peasant. To fight for independence meant then not only fighting the foreigner but also the landlords, and when you bested one you overcame the other. And this is what actually happened; this is what Uncle Ho and the Resistance and the Party brought to Vietnam. It made it possible to exist; life had some hope; a person could see a future and could have children with a good heart.

In addition to independence meaning existence and independence meaning land and land also meaning independence, there is this. The national feeling in Vietnam is very strong.

Vietnam was a nation hundreds of years before France and England and Italy and—permit me to mention it—before the

At the headquarters of the Liaison Committee of the DRV Army, formerly the home of Mme. Nhu, the Colonel in charge talks to the visitors.

31

United States. Many have invaded Vietnam, but none have permanently conquered; always there was resistance and always the Vietnamese people remained as a people with their own language and their own habits and food and ideas—and their own history of resistance. This is why seeing our country torn apart—without the south, Vietnam is without its feet and legs—tears apart our heart.

Independence, land, national unity and integrity—these are the basic things. It is these things that mean everything to every patriot; these things *are* patriotism.

This building, now the headquarters of the Liaison Committee of the DRV Army, formerly was the quite lavish home of Madame Nhu. In this house she was born and here she grew up, the house of her father, a wealthy lawyer serving the French rulers. She is back with the French again, this time in Paris.

The Colonel in charge talks for nearly two hours; he discusses in detail the Geneva Agreement of 1954, subsequent history of its implementation, current military developments and—especially—the political, diplomatic and moral difficulties and isolation of the U.S. government.

Saigon and the U.S. aggressors speak often now of DRV troops that they have encountered and engaged, but each time they say this they lie, he says. They prefer to believe—or prefer that others believe—that their military difficulties come to them from a regular army and a regular army that was the victor at Dien Bien Phu, but actually they come from the people's army inside South Vietnam, and that Army has not yet asked for others to come.

By the way, he adds, 160 million people have signed up to fight in Vietnam whenever asked to do so by the NLF or the

DRV. One hundred and sixty *million,* I ask? Yes, says the Colonel; over a billion now live in socialist countries, you know, and all of them support us, and 160 millions among their men have signed up for military duty here when called. You see, then, he adds, that the "strategic reserves" of the people of Vietnam are ample!

The Colonel comments at length and again in detail concerning the ferocious and atrocious bombings by the U.S. airforce. President Johnson, he recalls, once said that only steel and concrete are being bombed and that steel and concrete do not bleed, but President Johnson was not speaking truly. Human beings have been blasted and burned, cities have been bombed and not once but time and again, some more than ten times. And thousands have been killed in the DRV as a result, and each man, woman, and child so killed did bleed— exactly as people who are not Asians would bleed.

The Colonel noted that phosphorus shells had been used regularly but that after world-wide and repeated protests their use had been stopped. Would it not be possible for protest to stop the use of napalm bombs, absolutely barbarous weapons of mass slaughter?

The DRV would welcome an offer by American physicians and nurses to help heal the wounded; perhaps some U.S. doctors and nurses would want to "put their names down" for such service? We would welcome this for we know that it is not American doctors and workers and teachers and ordinary folk who want to bomb and destroy our country and we carefully distinguish between the present rulers of America and the vast majority of the American people.

Next to me is a young woman in her twenties; she stands about 4 feet 10 inches. She wears many medals, is a Hero of the NLF, has been in 33 engagements and is outstanding as

A Hero of the NLF, decorated many times for valor in battle; she is also a crack organizer and political leader.

a political leader and mass organizer. Except for the medals and her diminutiveness she reminds me of any of hundreds of young women college students back home—and of one such student in particular.

When Diem took the land back from the peasants, when he arrested former Resistance fighters in my village, we protested, she told me. But the repression grew. Always we demonstrated and petitioned; we did what we could politically.

But Diem wanted no politics, he wanted slavery. And when he carried his guillotine to our village and tortured men and women with boiling water and needles under their nails and began herding us into "hamlets" we had only two choices: Submission and slavery, or resistance and fighting for freedom. We Vietnamese have faced such choices before and we have never hesitated in the past and did not hesitate this time either. We could not do otherwise and we think that you, too, would have done as we did. How could anyone do otherwise? Foreigners came back, independence was gone, the land was gone and we could no longer live this way.

We had nothing but stones and bamboo sticks at first, and these are what we used. Then we captured guns and we organized and grew and now we are strong and many and well-trained and we will never stop fighting until the armed foreigners leave and independence comes back. Then again there will be land for the tillers and food for our mouths and schools for children—as already there are in our liberated areas. We will win back Vietnam for ourselves and run it for ourselves. We are Vietnamese and this is the way it should be and will be.

In our province, she said, Diem had made so many corpses they reached the mountain tops and he had spilled so much blood the rivers ran red. We young ones said we will not submit and we rose up. We will have independence. We cannot submit. What do you think? Do you not see? Would you not do as we have done if this had happened to you and those you love?

Those were the words of this recent teenager, this veteran soldier, this veteran mass leader, this fearsome threat to the Strategic Air Command and the mighty Pentagon.

Late December and early January, 1965-1966, the Hanoi Theatrical Troupe of the Democratic Republic of Vietnam was traveling through the countryside. Each of the provincial centers has a good theater and there for three or four days performances are offered. Not only the townspeople but also the peasant population stream through the doors and get the special feeling when the curtain rises.

Among Western playwrights the works of four are being offered this season in this fearsome country, in this land of darkness and tyranny, this land of machiavellian Communists who keep provoking a good-natured and liberty-loving Texan with his friend who has a computer instead of a heart.

This season the Troupe is showing to the workers and peasants of the Democratic Republic of Vietnam the creations of Shakespeare, George Bernard Shaw, Ibsen and O'Casey. What portentous news for Washington!

Earlier I mentioned that Twain has become a well-known friend to the people of the DRV since what they absurdly call "liberation"— i.e., since they compelled the French bosses to leave and all other kinds of bosses to behave themselves as though they were human beings. Note was taken also of the fact that soon Albert Maltz will be read in the cities and villages of this Asian land.

Maltz will be joining an august company, in which not only Sam Clemens sits. Already familiar to hundreds of thousands in this land regularly bombed by bright young men from the United States are: Whitman—he in particular, I was told; Faulkner, Caldwell—Erskine not Taylor; the old convict, O. Henry; Jack London, and—another particular favorite whose books cannot be printed in great enough copies— Hemingway.

Three things people carry in this benighted land: tools, rifles, books.

4. The Peace Committeeman

It is the invitation of the Vietnam Peace Committee that brought me here. With one of the members I have had hours of talk but always it was business—always he was explaining the history of his country, of the resistance against the French colonialists, against the Japanese fascists and now against the U.S. aggressors. Or he would explain the structure of government, and the nature of the urban and rural economy, or something about the traditional and modern culture of Vietnam, and the differences among Vietnamese now as to which was preferable or how the two might be blended or whether they should be or not, etc. "You know how writers and artists can talk," he says with a smile, being himself a poet and composer of distinction.

An interview with leaders of the Vietnam Peace Committee. Its President, a lay Buddhist leader, is on sofa next to author. Note the Catholic priest in the left foreground and the bonze at right foreground.

In the West, or at least in my country, I remark, it is not unusual for them to talk at great length, but often at home they talk about themselves. Yet of you I know almost nothing, I add, and others had to tell me that you write music and poetry and just the other day I have learned that you are the translator of Mark Twain. How in heaven's name, I ask, did you ever put into Vietnamese *Huckleberry Finn?* It was not easy, he admits, and I am far from sure that I was successful.

Of course I kept trying to get my friend's story and in time I think I learned something. At any rate let me tell you as much as I did find out.

This peace committeeman, who is fluent in Russian, French and English and who writes songs and oratorios and choral works—and is now working on an opera ("but I fear it is beyond my poor powers")—reaches his 43rd birthday in January of 1966.

He was born on a boat and on that boat he lived his first seven years. So he grew up almost like a fish, he says. The nearest he ever came to boasting was to confess that he was a good swimmer.

Where he was raised is the most beautiful part of Vietnam— "this I say with no hesitation at all." Its name in English is Islands of the Descending Dragon and there are six thousand of them. I fear I did not hear correctly: you said 6,000? Yes, there are 6,000 and I know each one like the palm of my hand. It is so beautiful there; each little isle has its own features, its own shape, its own reflection and the sun and the moon hit each in a certain way. It is beautiful.

What explains their name? Well, like practically everything else in Vietnam it has to do with fighting aggressors—for you know we have been doing this for 2,000 years. Legend has it that at the time of the invasion from the Chinese feudalists,

At the Historical Museum in Hanoi—original wooden piles used in Haiphong harbor, about 800 AD, to block Chinese feudalist invaders.

some were coming to our land by ships and they were approaching Haiphong. God sent a great dragon from heaven to protect our coast and this dragon spat out these islands and they were obstacles to the invaders. With their help we were finally able to save our coast and then rid our country of the interlopers. At that time, of course, it took us several generations rather than several years as with the French and the Japanese—and we think it will not take quite so long with the Americans either.

Living was too hard on the boat; there was not enough to eat. When I was eight years old I found myself living with an uncle, a fisherman, who lived on the mainland. I helped him and worked hard but there was a little more food. So I lived until I was 17, and I learned what I could on my own mostly— with the French, education was not for the Vietnamese, especially not workers or fishermen.

At the age of 17, I struck out on my own and went to work in the coal mines of Haiphong. It was fierce but I grew up. Then many of us were fired by the French boss and finally I found work, on the night shift, in a zinc factory. This was worse than the coal mines and I made barely enough to keep alive. After six months of it I returned to visit my family, and my father did not recognize me at first. He then told me I must leave that zinc hell and find something else for I was killing myself.

We Vietnamese, you know, take very seriously the advice of our elders—it is our way and we venerate the old—and therefore I left the zinc factory. I went to Hanoi and finally I found work as an assistant to a shoemaker. The pay was very, very low but the work was not exhausting; it was long but it was not killing.

Life was misery. Under the French, terror and indignity. Where you now are staying, he tells me, was the French area of the city and the other side of the lake was what was called the "indigenous quarters." No Vietnamese could go to the other side of the lake, except as a servant for the French. You understand, do you not? It was something like what you Americans call "jim crow." And every day people were arrested and the guillotine was rarely at rest.

It was misery and anarchy. Then, by 1944 the French had agreed to "give" our country to the Japanese and now both were on our necks, the Japanese fascists and the French colonialists. It was impossible, it was something you could not bear.

In that year of 1944 a buddy whom I had known in Haiphong met me and we again became friends. He it was who told me there was hope, there was a movement, there was a revolutionary effort. I joined quickly and I joined because it was not possible to go on this way and because I wanted to end misery and anarchy and because I knew nothing could be worse than the way things were and so I joined at once, as soon as they would let me.

When the Japanese left, or when most of them did, and the French remained and it was clear they intended to go back into business as before, we all rose together in the general rebellion of August 1945 and by September our independence was declared and our Republic was founded and the French said they agreed. But in a few months they came back with their battleships and planes and tanks and guns and so we did what we had to—we fought back.

So I was in the Army of National Salvation, in the War of the Resistance. It is then I met my wife; she was a nurse and we met in a first-aid station. But we were not then married and in 1949 she was captured by the French. She was their prisoner for one year and they tortured her. Our army people liberated the camp in which she was held and I saw her again and then she recuperated and she was back at her duty.

I learned inadvertently that the peace committeeman rose to the rank of major for I insisted that he tell me *something* of the fighting. The men fought well, he said. I can say that. For example, once my battalion, the one I commanded, was completely surrounded on all sides by French battalions. For five nights I did not sleep, but we did not surrender and on the sixth evening we made good our escape.

With peace in 1954, he married and now they have three sons—nine, seven, and five years old. They are not home now for they have been evacuated with many other children and we see them perhaps once a month. My wife misses them very much, he adds. With peace, too, I studied evenings and studied hard—languages and literature and music. Meanwhile I had studied society, too. When I joined the revolution I knew only that the misery and terror must end and that together all of us would end it but I knew nothing else. I knew nothing of economics or politics, nothing of the science, the theory of building a new society of equals and brothers. I knew nothing of Marxism, so I studied that hard, too.

What I want—what all of us want—is peace with a united, free and independent fatherland. I asked to work for peace and here I am on the peace committee staff. What we want is just. It is right for us to be independent and to make our own lives and we are going to do it no matter what it takes.

Most of this I learned as we traveled together, at night, south from Hanoi to the bombed areas—to the front. I felt I knew the committeeman now a little.

The Mayor of Nam Dinh welcomes the American guest.

5. In the City of Nam Dinh

After traveling some hours south from Hanoi, we arrive at the city of Nam Dinh in the province of Nam Ha. Nam Dinh is the third largest city in the Democratic Republic of Vietnam; in it live about 90,000 people. This is the battle-zone; eleven times in the past, U.S. planes have roared across the city dropping bombs and strafing with rockets and machine guns. In the province of which it is the capital live altogether about 1,700,000 people.

It is evening; the city committee greets us with flowers and the inimitable hospitality of the Vietnamese people. The person

Hayden, Lynd and Aphtheker view the ruins of the children's school in Nam Dinh, bombed by American pilots. The woman is one of the teachers and witnessed the attack.

whom we at home would call the Mayor apologizes for the somewhat inadequate and not absolutely impeccable condition of the building we are in—the city's headquarters have been damaged by U.S. aircraft.

One of the teachers is present and he expresses concern, for it has been necessary to move the school some distance from the city and this makes learning more difficult for the children. Still study goes on and trenches stand ready.

The leader of the Women's Committee expresses particular delight at seeing Americans and confirming that there is widespread opposition among the American people to the war. The bombings are barbarous, she told me, and not long ago our kindergarten was heavily damaged, at night, and not all the children could be evacuated in time—six had been killed. A two-month old infant had been orphaned in another attack and the Women's Committee was seeing to its upbringing.

Please understand what is happening and understand it well; of those killed in our city during the 11 times that American planes have bombed and strafed it, all have been either children or women or aged people. We know that President Johnson has said that his planes hit only steel and concrete and these do not bleed. He is not telling the American people the truth. His planes are hitting schools, kindergartens, pagodas, homes, factories. These are of steel and concrete and wood but inside them are human beings and human beings, including Asians, do bleed when bombs fall upon them.

Come, we shall show you and you will see for yourself.

We come to the kindergarten; one whole side of the roof and the first floor have collapsed. At the other end stands a gaping hole about 12 feet in width, made by rocket strafing. Two slogans still remain legible above a portal; these are translated for us: *To Bring Up Healthy Children,* says one; the other: *Educate Good Children.*

Outside the ruins of a pagoda destroyed by U. S. bombing missions over Nam Dinh. Repairs are under way.

45

The largest pagoda in the city—a big building with clearly distinguishable characteristics as a place of Buddhist worship—was hit on another occasion. Its interior still is a shambles with the religious objects destroyed; repair on the roof and exterior is well advanced. One of the monks who has greeted us points to the advanced repairs with great pride and says: "As soon as they destroyed it we began to repair it and if they destroy it ten times, we will repair it ten times."

The pride of the city is its large textile mill. Part of it was inherited from the French, but it has been many times expanded since liberation, and now 12,000 men and women, mostly women, work in it. Nothing is made here but textile materials, later to become clothing and bedding. It was bombed and strafed and the damage was considerable; some were killed and wounded. But the factory, now in dispersed form, goes on, three shifts, and producing more than ever. The night shift greets us; our job now is to produce as never before and to fight when we must. About the factory stand sub-machine guns and rifles.

Study goes on too. An integral part of the factory is its secondary technical school; it is named for Sékou Touré.

The people in this city have sharp and personal understanding of the meaning of a Johnson "peace feeler." Prior to bombings, U.S. aircraft often passed over the city telling the population of the latest "offer" by the President. It has reached the point where the children greet the falling of such leaflets as a sure sign of an impending bombing. On one occasion, the planes first dropped chocolate candy and even transistor radios —and later bombs.

We visit one of the gun emplacements outside the city. It is manned on a 24-hour basis by units not of the regular army but rather of the factory militia. In the darkness I make out

An anti-aircraft unit outside Nam Dinh— the girls who man the weapon are textile workers.

the two gray-clad figures at their posts within the emplacement and then as my vision adjusts I see that both are women. Yes, of course, the women workers and the men workers all take turns and are ready; we work day or night and we stand guard day or night.

This city's anti-aircraft units have shot down 28 aircraft.

The police of the city—this means people directing traffic and they carry no arms or weapons of any kind, not even a club—are all women.

I mention this to one of the women in the factory.

Yes, she says, most of the younger men are in the army. Then she adds: "You know here if a man strikes a woman it is a very serious crime."

I nodded and filed that away and then asked my peace committeeman about this.

This is Asia, you know, he begins. Here under the colonialists we all were oppressed but in those times the women were more than oppressed, they were enslaved. Hence, the beating of women by men, especially in the countryside, was most common. But not today; today nothing will bring a man a more severe penalty. Women now are not to be beaten and the Constitution affirms their equality, as the very first manifesto of the Party, in 1930, promised that this would be realized when workers and peasants held power. Now they do and now people do not beat each other and men do not hit women.

He went on, thinking of something related: You noticed that our police carried no weapon and no club. No, under the French we had enough of police with their clubs, beating us. Now our police direct traffic and do not have clubs.

Discussion with Father Dang Yuan Tu, 75-year-old Roman Catholic priest, in Nam Dinh.

The province of Nam Ha is heavily populated by Roman Catholics; they number 250,000. And in the city of Nam Dinh many live also. The largest structure in the city, in fact, is the Roman Catholic Church—so far it has not been damaged.

It is evening—one travels only at night. I ask to see the oldest priest and am introduced to a man of 75 years, Father Dang Yuan Tu.

Sixty years I have been in the Church, he says. In the old days—with the French—the Church was not free and now it is.

What do you mean, Father?

In the old days, early mass was for the French and not for us; we had to go to late mass. In the morning, soldiers guarded the church doors with guns and would not let us enter; only they, only the French, could enter.

Why was that, Father?

Why—why to keep us apart and to make us feel like intruders in our own home. They had two Christs in those days —one for the Vietnamese and one for the French.

I say, it is like in my country, Father. At home we have a Black Christ and a White Christ. Really, he says, I see. Then, abruptly: Why is it the Americans are bombing my city? What have we done to the Americans? Can you explain it to me? I do not understand. Why do they come here time after time and bomb this city? It is so cruel; it is inhuman. Can you tell me why it is?

My hosts come and tell me we must leave. There is an alert; they are forty miles away and we are not sure but it is not safe. I beg to be allowed to remain, but they will have none of it and I must leave. We say goodbye—the old priest and this American Communist deep in the heart of crucified Vietnam. I ask the Father's pardon for leaving so quickly—and to myself, I ask the Father's pardon for a million other things, too.

6. An American Pilot

Since the U.S. government has not seen fit to declare war upon the Democratic Republic of Vietnam but rather "only" to bomb it, those pilots who carry out these merciful missions and are brought down while doing so are considered not prisoners of war but rather apprehended criminals.

I had seen some of the results of the bombings here and being myself an American I am not unfamiliar with Americans; I wanted, therefore, to be able to talk with one of the captured pilots. There had been hints and more than hints in certain U.S. newspapers that such pilots were treated barbarously—even as badly as NLF prisoners are treated, perhaps!—and for this reason, too, I wanted to see and hear for myself.

The authorities agreed and a prisoner agreed; it later turned out in conversation with him that he had been told in general something of those who wished to meet with him.

With military authorities present, the pilot entered a rather large room in which three tables—laden with nuts, fruit, and tea—had been prepared. All were seated after the Americans had exchanged handshakes.

The pilot, though a prisoner for some months, looked altogether fit. His clothing was adequate and warm, though he added that it was difficult for the authorities to find sizes large enough for most Americans. The food was ample and not unpleasant; they took showers every other day. There were four English-language broadcasts a week to which they listened and an English-language newspaper that they read regularly. The cell was small and the biggest problem was lack of real exercise and the interminable hours. "It is no bed of roses, you can be sure, but it is all right. Frankly, I was quite surprised to be treated so well."

His plane had been hit at a high altitude—"I had plenty of time to look over the countryside as I came down." Within ten minutes militia units had captured him.

"They were well-trained and knew what to do. They offered me no violence and took me to a headquarters and processed me quickly and sent me on my way here (Hanoi)."

"Generally speaking they leave me alone—speak to me very little and have asked me very little."

He had been slightly injured but was now fully recovered and fit. He felt Okay. His spirits, under the circumstances, were high. He was fully in control of himself and was in good humor.

There had been some correspondence with his family and he would appreciate further word and welcome the opportunity to talk and visit. There was talk about baseball and football. And about the movement against the war in the United States. He wishes now he had paid more attention—before—to this Vietnam war and to the issues. Of course there were many viewpoints, but there sure was a great deal about the war and these people and their country that he had never known. It was clear how determined they were and how convinced they were that they were right.

Of course he missed the family and he missed being able to move around. Before in this job—his word—one could fly a thousand miles or more, spend the weekend at home and then get back to work on Monday. He prayed regularly that the war end. When he got home he'd like to be a teacher, that was quiet and steady and you could help kids grow up. He missed seeing his own grow up. What else was there, except seeing kids grow up? All kids? was interjected. Yes, he said with some pause and almost embarrassment, of course, all kids.

What was new in the peace movement? This was talked about and he was most interested. And civil rights? This, too, was discussed, and again his interest was real.

Did the folks back home take the war more seriously now? Were they really concerned? I tell you I pray for its end every day, every day, he went on. I imagine it's because people do not understand each other. It's all a matter of education, I guess. I really don't know. It will take many years, I guess. I certainly did not know about these people before I came here, that's for sure. They certainly believe in what they are doing and that's sure also.

He reverted again to his failure to pay any real attention to the war and the issues before "this happened." He wished he had so that he would understand more maybe. The main thing was to "end the mess." Of course, he was "working for the government" and so he had his own ideas and this was not the best place to talk about these at length.

It was getting quite late. Soon the talk dwindled. I noticed that he had eaten very little, a few nuts and had taken some tea. When he left he asked if he could take the cigarettes and fruit—several bananas and oranges—and nuts and candy with him. He was told "yes" and he did so.

Salutes were not exchanged. He said he had been happy to see us and that he was well and that he hoped we would all be able to get home soon. He wished he could come home now but, of course, he could not. He hoped there would be token releases perhaps. He had known about the release of Smith and McClure but he was shocked to hear that they had been tried by Army authorities, although he did not say anything about that news. But his shock was apparent and it was the only time he showed anything other than affability.

I admired his self-possession and his whole bearing under awful circumstances. He had done an atrocious "job" but its full quality did not seem to have penetrated or, if it had, he certainly kept it to himself. He knew there was much he did not know and he knew there was much about Vietnam and its people that he had no inkling of at all.

What a monstrous thing the present U.S. government had done! One sees this in a direct and fearful way when he looks at the bombings. And he sees it in another way—perhaps as fearful—when he looks upon the bombardiers. These are not the officers of the German army whom I had met as prisoners —cocky, arrogant, sneering, venomous, and most of all brutal. Somehow it made everything more horrible.

This was a "good Joe"—a good father, no doubt good at his "job," wondering why people did not "understand" each other, hoping somehow that sometimes "education" would end fighting, praying for an end to the "mess," knowing that there were important things that somehow he had never learned, saying absolutely nothing as to what had really brought him here— though interested, surely more than "before" in peace movements and civil rights activities. The American—well trained, vast technique at his disposal, affable, plenty of guts—and yet knowing practically nothing. And really with no ill-will in his heart, being sent by Pentagon and plutocracy to devastate a country some 10,000 miles from his home.

Markham indicted a ruling class that produced "the man with the hoe." How can one adequately indict the ruling class that has produced these smiling, ignorant men with bombs and rockets?

7. Vietnam's American Hero

Wherever one goes in the Democratic Republic of Vietnam, one sees the image of Norman Morrison, the American Quaker who immolated himself before the Pentagon last November in protest against U.S. aggression. Photographs and drawings of him adorn buildings, schools, churches, factories; streets have been named for him; and among the first questions asked of American visitors are those concerning Morrison, his wife, Ann, and their children.

I think this is a unique event in history; I mean, I do not know of another example wherein two countries are engaged in hostilities and one of the two makes of a citizen of the other its own decisive, popular hero. We have Lafayette, of course, but he was French and the French fought on our side in the Revolution; or the Chinese have Bethune, but he was a Canadian surgeon and Communist who assisted them in their revolutionary battles.

But the entire Vietnamese people have taken Norman Morrison and his family to their hearts.

Indicative of this is the fact that the poem "Emily, My Child" (Morrison's little daughter) is *the* poem in the Democratic Republic of Vietnam. Everyone seems to know it by heart. It has been set to music and is sung and listened to by tens of thousands.

This has come about because of two deep characteristics of the people of the DRV: First, an acute consciousness of internationalism, and second, a profound sense of humanism.

As to the internationalism, it is essential to a people who, having suffered foreign aggression so often and for so many generations, have had to distinguish between the rulers of the nations guilty of the aggression and the masses living within those nations. This was so with the Japanese and with the French and now with the Americans, notwithstanding the untold atrocities being committed by the U.S. government.

As to the sense of humanism, it is most difficult to put into words. But it is quite real and palpable, nevertheless, to one who is there. The Vietnamese are very quick to smile and to laugh; not ashamed to weep; and expectant of friendship and kindness. One of the sources of their humanism is the deep suffering; such profound and mass suffering, and resistance, uplifts the moral tone and quality of a people.

And there is this too—a sense of kinship. Every Vietnamese feels himself as being a member of the same family. This is part of the meaning of *Uncle Ho,* the title everyone uses for the President of the Republic. And it is a part of the infinite crucifixion of this people. For the separation into a north and a south is the same as the separation of wife and husband, or mother and child. It goes deeper than the separation of a nation whose thousands of years of history have been marked, above all, by a passion for unity and independence. It is really, quite literally, the separation of family.

At any rate, here is the poem that everyone knows in the *terrible* Democratic Republic of Vietnam; and it is written by a Secretary of the Central Committee of that Republic's Workers Party—one of those whom our *free* press, State Department and Pentagon keep talking about as the hard-core, robot-like, dehumanized Communist leaders:

The statue of "a thousand eyes and a thousand hands" in the Historical Museum in Hanoi.

EMILY, MY CHILD

by *To Huu*

"Emily, come with me
So when you're grown up
you will know the way."
"Where are we going, Daddy?"
     "To the banks of the Potomac."
"What do you want me to see, Daddy?"
      "I want you, dear, to see the Pentagon."
"Dearest child, with your wondering eyes,
Dearest child, with your shining hair."

Washington . . .
Twilight of souls
Still living or having lived.
Blaze high, truth, blaze high!
Reveal the piled-up crimes.
Humanity is outraged!
Johnson, dollar devil of our world,
How dare you borrow the mantle
Of Christ, or the saffron robe of Buddha!

McNamara,
Where are you hiding? In the crypts
Of your vast five-cornered house—
A corner for each continent?
You hide away from the fires you ignite
As an ostrich hides his head in the sand.

Look this way!
For this one moment, look at me,

Not just a man with a child in his arms.
I am Today itself,
And this, my Emily, is all our tomorrows.
Here I stand
Summoning the great heart of America,
To rekindle on the horizon
The beacon of justice.

Brood of the devil,
In whose name
Do you send the big bombers,
The napalm and the poison gas,
Straight from the White House
To Vietnam?
To murder peace and a nation's freedom,
To burn down hospitals and schools,
To kill people who know nothing but love,

To kill children on their way to school,
To kill fields that bloom with flowers and crops in every season,
To kill the flow of poetry and art and song?
In whose name
Do you bury American boys in coffins?
Young men, tall and strong,
Who might be tapping the powers of nature
To bring happiness to man?
In whose name do you send us to the jungles,
To the spike pits, to the resistance swamps,
To villages and towns which turn into fortresses,
Where day and night the earth shakes and the sky rocks?
Our Vietnam, this far-off land
Where little boys are heroes,

58

Where hornets are trained to fight,
Where flowers and fruits become weapons.

"Emily, my darling,
It's getting dark.
I cannot take you home tonight.
When the fire is over,
Mother will come and fetch you.
Will you give her a hug and kiss
For me?
And tell her
　　"Daddy went gladly, don't be sad!"

Washington,
Twilight of souls
Still living or having lived,
Now my heart burns at its brightest,
My blazing body
Becomes the torch of truth!

8. *Interview with the Prime Minister*

We received word that Prime Minister Pham Van Dong of the Democratic Republic of Vietnam happily granted our request and would be delighted to talk with "the Americans."

In the morning of January 5, we went to his residence, formerly the residence of the French Governor-General of Indochina.

The Prime Minister, unaccompanied, hurried down several stone steps and greeted us. He shook hands vigorously and invited us into a large and comfortable room.

About his throat was a scarf; he looks all of his 60-odd years. Rather dark-complexioned, slightly above the average height here, a very high forehead, serious eyes, but the ready smile that is quite characteristic of the Vietnamese—men and women and children.

After inquiring about our health and expressing concern lest our trip cause us difficulties upon returning home, he rather quickly began talking about the urgent questions facing his— and our—country and therefore the world.

This Prime Minister, like so many in the present-day world that has been so swiftly revolutionized, had spent many years in various prisons. He was a founder, in 1930, of the Communist Party of Indochina, the direct ancestor of the present Workers Party of Vietnam. He was in the midst of the fierce struggles against French colonialism and Japanese fascism and has been the Prime Minister of this Republic ever since its independence was affirmed in 1945.

And now Prime Minister of a country regularly bombed and

strafed by the U.S. Air Force, while that portion of his own nation from which he comes—the Prime Minister's home was near Pleiku—undergoes the crucifixion brought it by over 200,000 American troops.

Of course we desire peace more than any other people for we are experiencing the full horrors of modern war, he begins. But our greatest passion is for independence; this is not rhetoric, it is reality. Ask even our children, they know very well what the fighting is about.

We grieve for the suffering of our children and our women, of our young and aged. We are a sentimental people, a people full of feelings and easily moved. We think of our nation as one family. We call our President "Uncle Ho," and this expresses something of that feeling. We feel a pain in our heart because of our country's suffering. And I am myself from the South.

We think we desire peace much more than does President Johnson. But at what cost must we have peace, according to him? At the cost of slavery.

Here is the problem. We must have our independence. We, every last one of us, would rather die than be enslaved. If you American people were in our position you would do the same. I am sure you would—I think highly of you and your traditions and I know you would.

President Johnson speaks of the honor of the United States —can it be to throw bombs and rockets upon this country? Is that honorable?

As long as the aggressor remains on our soil we will fight and the peoples of the world—including, I am sure, more and more American people—will support us. What we are doing is right. We are ready to sacrifice everything for our just cause for if we do not win we will have nothing.

When a people is thus inspired, they fear nothing, he continues. Such a people can work miracles. Always in my life, I tell you frankly, I have been surprised at what the people can accomplish. There is nothing they cannot do.

Almost 200,000 U.S. troops with every modern weapon are upon our homeland and bombers have thrown tons and tons of explosives upon us, but now we are stronger than before and we are more united than ever. There is no hatred between our peoples—we have no ill will toward American people. On the contrary, we know and respect their splendid traditions.

In response to questions he makes clear that though President Johnson has recently—in the course of his latest and noisiest "peace campaign"—said that he was knocking on every door and actively pursuing peace, he has not knocked upon the door of the Democratic Republic of Vietnam! Surely this is a peculiar way to actively pursue peace, I think to myself! To "knock on every door" except the one door that must be knocked upon by President Johnson.

The need is for the United States government to give up its present aggressive policy, the Prime Minister continues. There are many complicated questions involved but the biggest question is perfectly simple. The United States government must make up its mind to change its present policy toward Vietnam; it must decide to cease its aggression against this nation and make up its mind that it must live in the same world with an independent Vietnam. With this decision everything else will be solved and without it nothing will be solved—no matter what the maneuvers.

The world daily becomes smaller—peace was never more necessary in the history of mankind. History is bringing the peoples of the world closer. History is bringing about the emancipation of nations and of peoples. I am a Marxist-Leninist and I believe in the course of history's laws. Those who stand in their way will be defeated. But whether or not one agrees with this, nations must be independent and aggressions against them must cease.

Please, if you should see President Johnson, ask him why is he bombing my country? Let him explain exactly how the Democratic Republic of Vietnam is threatening the United States of America?

Johnson is learning that for Americans to fight a war in Asia is to court disaster. Such fighting is not favorable to the armed forces. And in fighting an unjust war soldiers do not fight well and that is to their honor really.

The U.S. government must want peace. Now it does not. That is the heart of the matter. A change must come—the moment will come and I hope it comes soon, but until it comes the problem is not going to be solved. We will fight until it comes and not one second longer.

The highest sentiment of our age is fraternity among peoples. And our age is the one that will be marked by the triumph of that sentiment.

The Prime Minister walks us about the gardens, and then as he bids farewell and shakes hands, he says that we must have peace in this era, we must have world peace, and with independence for the peoples there will be peace for the peoples.

PART TWO

Our Insane Policy

On our way home, I get the free world press again—and the insanity again. In the *Herald-Tribune* of December 29, Ted Sell writes from Washington that the bombings of North Vietnam have not succeeded in dislocating its society. He reports that in the Pentagon, many are saying, quoting Mr. Sell: "Now, only massive attacks, perhaps with nuclear weapons, could cause such immediate dislocation."

Before I came to the target area, I had read such things and shuddered. But now that I have been to that area—with the kids on the air-raid shelters, with the 75-year old priest, with the women selling flowers—now it is—I do not know what to say—it is like a nightmare.

I looked upon concentration camps in 1945; I saw the ovens and when our outfit arrived, the places still stank. I saw it but I could not believe it. That was a nightmare. But we had fought against it, we had been on the side of the inmates. If that was a nightmare, what was this? Now, the crematoria are made in the United States and are portable and are called napalm bombs and phosphorus shells—and journalists are coolly writing of "dislocation" with massive attacks using nuclear weapons!

I read in *Newsweek* of January 10, 1966, that Bob Hope was in Saigon entertaining 10,000 troops with his inimitable wit. The magazine says: "They roared when Hope called the U.S. bombing raids on North Vietnam 'the best slum clearance project they ever had.' " I remember how we forced some of the SS officers to go through the concentration camps and we all filed through with handkerchiefs to our noses, and when we emerged into the air and the nazis dropped their handkerchiefs, I remember that some were laughing! The crematoria constituted one huge sewerage project to them, in which vermin—Jews, Communists, Slavs—were exterminated.

Professor Hans Morgenthau writes truly when he indicts this "senseless, hopeless, and brutalizing war." Dr. Benjamin Spock writes truly when he declares, of what U.S. armed might is doing in Vietnam: "When Hitler's armies used such tactics we called them atrocities."

The Peace Offensive

When Hitler's armies marched, he did not say but the world knew that he wanted the oil and coal, the wheat and iron of the Ukraine, that he wanted to annihilate the idea of popular sovereignty, that he sought to extirpate socialism. Such realistic considerations are scarce today in the noble rhetoric with which American-made atrocities are bedecked. But it was not always so. Thus, when the French were doing most of the fighting against the Vietnamese, the *New York Times* editorialized, February 12, 1950: "Indo-China is a prize worth a large gamble. In the north are exportable tin, tungsten, zinc, manganese, coal, lumber and rice, and in the south are rice, rubber, tea, pepper . . . ."

And a little later—but while the French still held the line— President Eisenhower permitted himself to express these thoughts, in his characteristic syntax, at the U.S. Governors' Conference, August 4, 1953:

"Now let us assume that we lost Indo-China. If Indo-China

goes, several things happen right away. The peninsula, the last bit of land hanging on down there, would be scarcely defensible. The tin and tungsten that we so greatly value from that area would cease coming. . . . So when the United States votes $400 millions to help that war, we are not voting a giveaway program. We are voting for the cheapest way we can to prevent the occurrence of something that would be of a most terrible significance to the United States of America, our security, our power and ability to get certain things we need from the riches of the Indo-Chinese territory and from Southeast Asia."

Lyndon B. Johnson, as President of the United States, tends to deliver himself of elevated prose, at least upon formal occasions, though at his order the armed forces deliver something other than prose. Still, one wonders whether the truer Lyndon B. Johnson was speaking when as a Congressman he said on the floor of the House, March 15, 1948: "No matter what else we have of offensive or defensive weapons, without superior air power America is a bound and throttled giant; impotent and an easy prey to any yellow dwarf with a pocket knife." Indeed, of the same order, one learns from the *New York Times* of January 29, 1966, that the President has rechristened one of his dogs. He now calls his male hound, Ho Chi Him. It is of some interest to note that while in Hanoi I was informed that President Ho Chi Minh was known to ride, at times, a jackass.

It is this chauvinism, this racism, colonialism, this parasitic appetite—as well as considerations of strategic position and future activities against other socialist lands—that lie at the base, I think, of the aggressive foreign policy now dominating Washington.

Whatever demagogic purposes may have prompted the issuance of President Johnson's Fourteen Points, and whatever devious intentions lay behind his much-trumpeted "peace offensive," at least their language and the verbiage of the "offensive" reflected some recognition of the need to respond to the mounting pressures for peace. That world public opinion, Vietnamese resistance, and U.S. public opinion played a part in inducing that "offensive" and that verbiage is all to the good.

The first point of the Fourteen-Point statement issued by President Johnson on December 27, 1965—acceptance of the Geneva Agreements—represents the essential point of both the National Liberation Front of South Vietnam and of the Democratic Republic of [North] Vietnam. If adhered to and implemented, it means an end to the war in Vietnam and the basis for a lasting peace in Southeast Asia.

The Geneva Agreement of 1954 was for the people of Vietnam what the Treaty of Paris of 1783 was for the people of the United States. Both represented treaties entered into after prolonged negotiations by defeated colonial powers—Great Britain and France—with the formerly colonial peoples—American and Vietnamese—who had won their independence through struggle.

The Geneva Agreement was a generous one offered by the victorious Vietnamese to the defeated French. Thus, though the Vietnamese had proposed that the temporary military line of demarcation be at the 15th parallel and the French at the 18th, the final Geneva Agreement set it at the 17th, representing a concession to the French not only of considerable territory but also of some two million people.

But this was agreed to and Geneva as a whole was signed by the Vietnamese because it contained the main things: The acceptance of the independence, unity and integrity of the Vietnam nation, affirmed the temporary non-political character of the split at the 17th parallel, required the withdrawal of all foreign troops from Vietnam, prohibited the future introduction of such troops, and set down procedures for the reunifica-

68

tion of Vietnam by 1956. And it was accepted by and the terms were carried out by the Vietnamese people because "Uncle Ho" asked them to do so—and Ho Chi Minh is to the Vietnamese what Washington, Lincoln, and Lenin taken together represent.

The Geneva Agreement terminated a "dirty war" waged for over eight years—1946-1954—by the French with the massive assistance of the United States.

It is universally acknowledged—as by former President Eisenhower, for example, in his *Mandate for Change,* and more recently by Arthur M. Schlesinger, Jr., in his account of the Kennedy years—that the 1956 elections were not held at the insistence of Saigon and Washington because, as was said at the time, it was certain that Ho Chi Minh would have emerged, in such elections, as the choice of the overwhelming majority of the Vietnamese people, in both the north and the south. (The figure cited by Eisenhower is an 80 per cent plurality for Ho Chi Minh.)

Nevertheless, since Geneva and since 1956, the DRV has tried repeatedly, though without success, to normalize relations between South and North Vietnam. Furthermore, in three important respects—as was emphasized to us during the journey by highest authorities—agreements already have been offered going further than the Geneva accord. Thus, the DRV—and since its founding in 1960, the NLF—have agreed to:

(a) the neutrality in foreign policy of the South Vietnam interim government;

(b) the broad, coalition character of such a government;

(c) a prolonged process for the peaceful reunification of North and South Vietnam, determined without outside interference by the people involved and confirmed by a general, free election.

None of these three points was in the Geneva Agreement. All—and this was, I repeat, emphasized in the course of our journey—illustrate, certainly in their own view, the moderation of the DRV approach. Surely their existence, undoubtedly unknown to the vast majority of Americans, refutes the Washington stereotype of the DRV and the NLF as intransigent and stubborn, not to say war-seeking.

The fact is that after 25 years of war no people on earth craves peace more than those in Vietnam. But those 25 years of war were inspired by the goal of the independence and integrity of the Vietnamese nation. This is an indispensable prerequisite. And let it be added that the very long experience of the Vietnamese people—covering thousands of years—has shown them that without independence, existence—quite literally, existence—becomes either impossible or unbearable. As just one example of what is meant: *In the single year, 1944, under the Japanese fascists and the French colonialists, two million Vietnamese died of starvation.*

Hence, without independence, it is passionately felt in Vietnam, any "peace" can only represent surrender and no one—least of all the United States, created in a war for independence—should demand or expect such abandonment.

It was independence, unity and national integrity which were the heart of Geneva, and many Vietnamese wonder if it is not because of this that the highest officials of the U.S. government—such as Secretary of State Dulles and President Eisenhower—expressed so low an opinion of the Geneva Agreement at the time of its signing.

If the first of the Fourteen Points of December 27 is meant in full seriousness, nothing else is necessary. That point means the recognition of Vietnamese independence, unity and national integrity, and it requires the removal of all foreign troops from

70

Vietnam. Let the first be solemnly affirmed and let the second process be begun and—my journey persuades me—peace is well on its way in Vietnam.

In this connection, however, it is necessary to observe that so universally respected a commentator as Walter Lippmann, in his column dated December 29, 1965, concludes: "I believe it a grave mistake to attempt to make permanent our military presence on the Asian mainland. . . . Making this artificial and ramshackle debris of old empires permanent and committing our lives and fortunes to its maintenance means, I believe, unending war in Asia." It is necessary also to observe that Tom Lambert, writing from Washington in the *New York Herald Tribune* of December 31—several days after the announcement of the Fourteen Points—notes that while the United States will accept "a nonaligned South Vietnam," nevertheless, the U.S. "will not let South Vietnam go to the Communists and will remain there militarily if necessary to preclude any such Communist takeover." This rules out the free and unfettered choice by the people involved. Furthermore, since it depends upon what Washington considers "Communist," it may well rule out anything to the Left of the present "Premier" of the Saigon regime—a pilot for the French and a man who has stated that his favorite hero is Hitler!

And Mr. Lambert went on in the same dispatch to quote the President's assistant, Mr. Bill D. Moyers, as repeating that the "basic" aim of the United States in Vietnam—as stated by President Johnson in Baltimore in April 1965—remains, namely, the U.S. "demands an independent South Vietnam securely guaranteed." But the central point of Geneva was the temporary character of the two-zone separation of Vietnam and the agreement as to the unity and sovereignty of Vietnam— not North and South, but Vietnam. One cannot affirm adher-

71

ence to Geneva and at the same time, with reason, insist that a "basic" demand is for a separate, independent and "non-Communist" South Vietnam!*

Clearly and correctly, I believe, the Vietnamese feel that their struggle is a just war for national independence. It is a continuation of an anti-colonialist and anti-imperialist effort waged against the Japanese, the French, the French-American and now the American governments.

Further, the struggle seeks not only the cause of the triumph of the national liberation of the Vietnamese people. In addition, such a victory would thwart the effort of the U.S. government to establish a military stronghold in Southeast Asia for purposes of conquest and exploitation in that area, and as a base for further assaults throughout Asia, thus clearly opening up the prospects of a general and even a Third World War.

The Vietnamese take very seriously the unanimous conclusions reached at the 1957 and 1960 conferences of the Workers' and Communist Parties of the world. There it was agreed that a prime task was to exert every effort to further the cause of national liberation and simultaneously to prevent world war. Both were viewed as two sides of the same anti-imperialist effort. The present struggle against the U.S. government's policy of aggression in Vietnam is held to be exactly that kind of effort.

* That this remains "basic" was made clear again in February 1966 in the testimony of General Maxwell D. Taylor before the Senate Foreign Relations Committee. Max Frankel, writing from Washington, in the *New York Times,* Feb. 18, 1966, commented: "Gen. Maxwell D. Taylor brought out in public today what other high officials here have made increasingly plain in private—namely that the United States' terms for peace in Vietnam are much stiffer than the offer of 'unconditional' negotiations has implied . . . to force the Communists to accept an independent and non-Communist South Vietnam. The Johnson Administration has never wavered in the pursuit of that objective."

72

It is, then, a fundamental issue in the central task of our era —the achievement of national liberation and the prevention of world war—i.e., the implementation of the policy of peaceful coexistence.

The Vietnamese insist upon distinguishing between the U.S. government and the American people. They value most highly the impressive efforts for peace being made by large and growing segments of the American public. It is a historical fact that the present degree of opposition to an actual war being conducted is without precedent and the relative absence of passionate support of such an actual war also is without precedent in the history of the United States.

Furthermore, the Vietnamese do not seek the defeat of the United States and do not conceive of themselves as capable of defeating the United States. That is, they are not waging war upon the United States and do not seek the destruction of our cities, let alone the capture of Washington. They are seeking only to defeat the American aggression upon their soil; they seek to defeat the American government's aggressive foreign policy insofar as that manifests itself in their country.

Certainly the aggressive war policy of the Johnson Administration has brought death and maiming to thousands of Americans, and these casualties will increase as the number of men committed increases and as the hostilities intensify. The policy has brought mass death and devastation to Vietnam.

The aggressive policy of the Johnson Administration threatens all social progress and democratic achievements in the United States; thus, there is a 3.2 per cent ceiling upon wage increases, but there is no ceiling at all for rates of profit by corporations—and these have reached all-time highs. There is impotence in the face of the murders of dozens of civil rights workers inside the United States, and the capacity to send almost a quarter of a million American soldiers thousands of miles from home to slaughter peasants and burn villages!

The Johnson policy of aggression threatens the American people with the kind of catastrophe that Hitler's policy of aggression did bring the German people.

The President of the United States speaks of our honor as a nation. Does it honor our nation to ravage a people who have done us no harm? Does it honor our nation to spread chemical poison upon the land and labor of Asian peasants? Does it honor our nation to turn children into beggars and women into prostitutes? Does it honor our nation to hurl phosphorus shells and napalm bombs upon the homes and the flesh of millions of men, women and children?

If to shout to the heavens in denunciation of such "honor" be treason, the present writer requests that his name be enrolled high upon the list of such traitors.

A reversal of the present aggressive foreign policy of the U.S. government is in the best interests of the people of Vietnam and of the United States, and of the entire world. Pressures for such a reversal are mounting everywhere and they are mounting here. Of course, here is the main responsibility.

What Price Patriotism?

Accusations abound, now that the nation is engaged in war, against the patriotism of those citizens who doubt its wisdom or legality or justice and insist upon expressing their doubts.

Recently, Senator Russell B. Long of Louisiana repeatedly affirmed his unswerving patriotism—though who had denied it was unclear—in a long speech on the floor of Congress (February 16, 1966). In what must be among the most delicious typographical errors—or verbal slips—in history, Senator

74

Long was quoted in the *New York Times,* the next day, this way:

"I swell with pride when I see Old Glory flying from the Capitol. I swell with pride when I see the flags around the Washington Monument. I swell with price when I see the American flag flying from the Senate Office Building."

In view of the widespread influence of the substance, if not the style, of the Senator's remarks it will not be amiss to comment briefly, with a couple of historical allusions, upon that substance.

One would not expect the Senator from Louisiana to note the special irony in the fact that his screaming-eagle harangue was made in the midst of Negro History Week—a week established in 1926 through the inspiration of the late Dr. Carter G. Woodson, and placed by him in the month of February because that was the birth-month of both Frederick Douglass and Abraham Lincoln. The two men, now dead for many decades, are safe from attacks of treason but it is appropriate to recall their statements concerning another war waged by the U.S. government—statements made while that war was going on.

Thus, Abraham Lincoln as a new Congressman from Illinois, was appalled by the Annual Message delivered by President Polk in January 1848, for much of it was devoted to a defense of the war then being carried on against Mexico—and in those dear old days, wars *were* declared. Abraham Lincoln said in the House, January 12, 1848, ". . . I cannot be silent, if I would." He could not contain himself, Lincoln explained, because the President's message, "is, from beginning to end, the sheerest deception." Mr. Lincoln permitted himself to express the belief that the President "is deeply conscious of being in the wrong—that he feels the blood of this war, like the blood of Abel, is crying to Heaven against him."

The President, young Lincoln went on, in words of fire, is "trusting to escape scrutiny, by fixing the public gaze upon the exceeding brightness of military glory—that attractive rainbow, that rises in showers of blood—that serpent's eye, that charms to destroy. . . . How like the insane mumbling of a fever-dream, is the whole war part of his late message . . . urging the national honor, the security of the future, the prevention of foreign interference, and even, the good of Mexico herself, as among the objects of the war. . . . His mind, tasked beyond its power, is running hither and thither, like some tortured creature, on a burning surface, finding no position. . . . He is a bewildered, confounded, and miserably perplexed man. God grant he may be able to show, there is not something about his conscience, more painful than all his mental perplexity."

The same month and year, Frederick Douglass wrote in his Rochester, N. Y., newspaper, *The North Star,* of "the present disgraceful, cruel, and iniquitous war." It was a war, Douglass continued, characterized by "grasping ambition, tyrannic usurpation, atrocious aggression, cruel and haughty pride." Concluded Douglass, in words at least as piercing as those simultaneously being used by Lincoln:

"The groans of slaughtered men, the screams of violated women, and the cries of orphan children, must bring no throb of pity from our national heart, but must rather serve as music to inspire our gallant troops to deeds of atrocious cruelty, lust and blood."

In these more tame and less passionate days—in these benumbed years—language like this rarely appears; at any rate, perhaps enough has been said to show the deeply-seeded traditions within the United States of expressing decided and even fierce opposition to the policy of the government, including that policy when it eventuates in war.

On January 16, 1966, Secretary of State Rusk was explaining to the House Foreign Affairs Committee some of the difficulties faced by one in his position. He commented: "Only one-third of the world's population are asleep at any one time. The other two-thirds are awake and probably committing some mischief."

It is not often that this writer finds himself in agreement with Dean Rusk but in this case, having recently returned from that portion of the globe wherein live two-thirds of the human race, it seems to me he is correct, even though his characteristically chauvinist method of expression—"mischief"—grates on my nerves.

The Rationale of Aggression

The Domino Theory

Several of the most commonly urged arguments in favor of the Johnson policy may be briefly noted. One is the so-called "domino" theory, insisting that only the present policy prevents other states from "falling away" from the United States. I believe that the truth is exactly the contrary; I think the evidence demonstrates that the Johnson policy—and especially as that policy dramatized itself with the commencement of the bombings of the DRV in February 1965—has flung all the dominoes upon the floor and that only its reversal will make possible replacing them.

Thus, the thoroughly experienced American newspaperman, Joseph Barry, writes from Paris (in *The Progressive,* February 1966): "Everywhere in Europe the Vietnam war has poisoned whatever else has been positive in American policy. It has reduced to nil everything but our military leadership and made nonsense our claims to moral law and international order."

77

If this is true in Europe—and numerous commentators confirm Mr. Barry's view—one can well imagine the situation in Asia, Latin America and Africa. Certainly in Cambodia, India, Burma, Pakistan, Japan, the Philippines, the Vietnam policy of the United States has embarrassed governments and infuriated the populace. Said the entire distinguished editorial board of that leading "Christian Journal of Opinion," *Christianity and Crisis,* in an essay entitled, "We Protest the National Policy in Vietnam": "Our nation is becoming increasingly lonely in the world, losing or embarrassing European, African and Asian allies, and building a legacy of hatred and resentment for 'neo-colonialism.' " (March 7, 1966).

Chinese "Aggression"

Another much-repeated argument holds that it is really Chinese "aggression" that explains the selfless activity of the U.S. government in Southeast Asia. That government has committed a quarter of a million troops to combat there for no sordid or material or territorial or economic reason; no, the reason is that we seek to hurl back Chinese aggressiveness.

I think that this argument being urged in the face of the incontrovertible facts concerning Chinese-American relations can only be explained on the basis of a complete loss of any sense of irony and perhaps a kind of madness induced by the racism that permeates so much of ruling-class thinking in the United States.

Consider what would be the reaction in the United States if it were this country rather than China that was surrounded by scores of army, air and naval bases; if 300,000 Chinese combat troops were in Canada and in Mexico rather than 300,000 U.S. combat troops in Korea and Vietnam; if a Chinese fleet regularly patrolled and at times interdicted the American coasts, rather than U.S. warships that openly so treat the coast of China; if Chinese military aircraft periodically flew over U.S. territory for the purpose of intelligence and reconnaissance, rather than what is today the fact—that U.S. military aircraft so behave over the territory of China; if China intervened in an American civil war and, favoring one of the two sides, helped the favored one to retain in its possession Staten Island, Nantucket, and the Florida Keys, rather than what is today true— i.e., the U.S. making it possible for Chiang to exist and to retain Quemoy, Matsu and Taiwan.

In connection with the charge of Chinese "aggression," the Korean War frequently is invoked. What, however, are the facts in connection with that war and Chinese-American relations?

It was only after U.S. (UN) forces advanced north of the 38th parallel—separating South and North Korea—that the Chinese issued any warnings at all of their possible intervention. As MacArthur kept moving North these warnings increased. When MacArthur announced that his goal was the Yalu River "by Christmas" and "home by New Year's," the Chinese government called in the Indian Ambassador, K. M. Pannikar—who writes of this in his memoirs—and told him that Peking having no relations with Washington was requesting New Delhi to inform Washington that the announced goal of MacArthur was one which the Chinese government could not and would not allow. It was pointed out that the Yalu is to China what the St. Lawrence is to the United States; that it constituted an actual boundary of China and that the power from its waters served hydroelectric plants inside China as well as inside Korea.

When this information was passed on to Washington and from there to General MacArthur, the latter assured President Truman that he knew "the oriental mind," that it understood only force and that he—MacArthur—was "certain" China was bluffing.

As the U.S. (UN) forces approached the Yalu, 150,000 Chinese troops entered the struggle, sent MacArthur's forces reeling southward and drove them to the 38th parallel. At that point the Chinese troops stopped and soon thereafter withdrew from Korea. There have been since and are now no Chinese troops inside Korea; but there are today about 60,000 U.S. combat troops in that still-divided country.

Here again, the facts demonstrate Chinese restraint, not Chinese aggressiveness. Overall, the rationalization used by the Johnson Administration for its war against Vietnam—that is, to prevent Chinese "aggression"—is a classic example of "thief shouting thief."

The "Appeasement" Argument

From Vice President Humphrey and President Johnson one hears repeatedly that supporting the present war in Vietnam reflects an understanding of the "lesson of Munich" and a rejection of the disastrous path of appeasement. The American people are incessantly told that appeasing aggressors does not satisfy or restrain them but rather strengthens and encourages them. Hence, now in Vietnam (and in the Dominican Republic!) they must be stopped and this must be done no matter what the cost or the danger involved.

Again, a fundamental misconception is at the root of this argument. The indigenous quality of the revolutionary movements in Asia is decisive; they are in fact revolutionary movements and reactionary efforts to suppress them bring about civil wars. In these wars colonial powers—like Japan, France, Britain, the Netherlands—regularly have intervened; and so has and so is the United States. When the Dutch sought to suppress the Indonesian struggle for independence, the only foreigners fighting in Indonesia were—the Dutch. When the French sought to suppress the Vietnam struggle for independence, the only foreigners fighting in Vietnam were—the French. Now that the Americans are seeking to suppress the Vietnam struggle for independence, the only foreigners fighting in Vietnam are—the Americans (plus, most recently, some South Koreans, paid by the United States, and a token force of New Zealanders and Australians).

To equate such events with the steady violent advances of the fascist powers—Italy, Germany and Japan—during the 1930's is to equate George Washington with Count Metternich.

Furthermore, the whole point of Munich—and it is allegedly to avoid "another Munich" that American youths are fighting ten thousand miles from home—was not appeasement in any accurate definition of the term. This word carries with it the idea that what was given to Hitler was yielded grudgingly. Nothing can be further from the truth.

Hitler was created, financed, built up by German monopoly capital and simultaneously by the ruling circles of France, Great Britain and the United States. They did not *yield* to Hitler—they *lavished* upon Hitler. They not only gave him what he wanted; they gave him—as his correspondence and recorded conversations have since revealed—actually more than he expected and sometimes more than he had requested. They gave him naval equality; the legal right to rearm; a remilitarized Rhineland; the Saar; Danzig; Memel; Austria. They gave him (and Mussolini) victory in Spain. We know now that they were seriously offering him the former Kaiser's colonies in Africa. And in Munich—against the protests of the USSR and the Left throughout the world—they gave him all Czechoslovakia, with its first-rate industry, its superb munitions works, its magnificent fortifications, and its eastern finger touching the Soviet Union.

This was a policy of emboldening and encouraging. Hitler was *made* into a giant as a *policy* of international monopoly with the purpose of using that giant to spearhead the military destruction of the Soviet Union and thus, once and for all, to "finish" with socialism.

The so-called appeasers of yesterday are the aggressors of today. The Municheers of the past are the bombardiers of the present. The Hearst press that today leads the cry for war in the name of resisting appeasement was the same press that opened its pages to the writings of Mussolini and Goering regularly throughout the thirties. It was to the *New York Daily News* that President Roosevelt symbolically gave the nazi Iron Cross and he did that in recognition of its real Munich spirit; it is the *Daily News* which again leads the hounds of war.

Yesterday's "appeasers" are today's aggressors because yesterday and today they hated and hate socialism; because yesterday and today they preferred and prefer reaction; because yesterday and today they did and they do opt for fascism rather than live in peace with socialism and permit the masses in the world to work out for themselves a destiny of creative living, real abundance and full sovereignty.

Is There a Civil War?

Lately, the Johnson Administration has been seeking to convince the American people that there is no genuine struggle within South Vietnam at all; that the National Liberation Front of South Vietnam is a figment and a misnomer and that there is nothing of even a civil war quality in the fighting there. Indeed, Secretary McNamara in his testimony before the Senate Foreign Relations Committee on March 3, 1966, stated the

82

Times the next day, "devoted much of his formal statement to controverting the argument that the Vietnam conflict was a civil war."

This was its character, however, in the 1950's with this proviso; even then most of the money and materiel used by the Saigon authorities came from the United States. U.S. intervention has increased, of course, throughout the 1960's and by the end of 1964—despite colossal U.S. assistance—the Saigon regime had been defeated militarily.* It is because of this that U.S. military intervention became massive—by land, air and sea—beginning in 1965, until at the end of the first quarter of 1966, there are about 250,000 U.S. combat troops on the ground in Vietnam and they are backed up by the entire 7th Fleet, plus the Strategic Air Command and tens of thousands of maintenance and supply troops in Okinawa, Japan, the Philippines, Guam, Hawaii and the continental United States.

One may, then, now agree with McNamara when he says the war in Vietnam is no longer a civil war; it is now predominantly a war waged by the United States against the people in South and North Vietnam with the formal support of its Saigon

* It now appears quite clear that late in 1964 or very early in 1965 President Ho Chi Minh made still another request to Washington that discussions looking toward peace be undertaken. James A. Wechsler in his *N. Y. Post* column (March 10, 1966) declares "further inquiry documents the point that the venerable chieftain of Vietnam . . . had indicated through intermediaries his readiness to confer with President Johnson in Rangoon." Wechsler says Washington rejected this, believing that news of such a meeting would complete the disintegration of what was left of the Saigon regime; and that *the next day* Washington began the bombing of the DRV!—accidentally, Wechsler thinks! Rejecting any discussions, and resorting to the bombing of the DRV—while the Prime Minister of the USSR was visiting that Republic, too—demonstrates Washington's decision in face of Saigon's complete collapse, to "take over the war," to expand it, and to turn it more openly into a war waged by the U.S. government against the Vietnamese people.

puppets. It has reached the point where those puppets themselves admit 113,000 desertions from their own army in a single year; it has reached the point where, as the American press admits, major military campaigns are undertaken now by U.S. forces without even informing the Saigon authorities that they impend!

As for the indigenous reality of the NLF, the evidence is abundant and altogether persuasive. This is why, as Norman Cousins wrote in *The Saturday Review* (February 27, 1965): "In briefing of new U.S. military personnel, the point is stressed that most Vietnamese are either sympathizers with or secret members of the Vietcong." This is why most of the territory of South Vietnam is now in the hands of the so-called rebels (*New York Times* maps show this to amount to 80 per cent of the area) and why the fullest NLF control is exercised precisely at the lowest extremity of South Vietnam, i.e., the Mekong river delta region—about one thousand miles away from the southernmost tip of North Vietnam!

"All the evidence," declared the *St. Louis Post-Dispatch,* editorially (February 15, 1965), "points to a high degree of local sympathy or outright support for the Vietcong as a major element in its success." In the Fall of 1963 David Halberstam, then in South Vietnam, wrote from the Camau peninsula—as far south as one can go and still be in Vietnam—"almost the entire population is Communist." He added: "The people pay taxes to the Vietcong, send their children to Vietcong schools, and their young men into Vietcong military ranks" (*New York Times,* September 16, 1963).*

---

* Why things stand as Mr. Halberstam describes them was indicated in the remarkable sentence uttered on Feb. 26, 1966, by Henry Cabot Lodge, U.S. Ambassador in Saigon: "For years now in Southeast Asia, the only people who have done anything for the little man at the grassroots—to lift him up—have been the Communists." (*New York Times,* Feb. 27, 1966.)

Even General Paul D. Harkins, then Commander of U.S. forces in South Vietnam, was quoted in this fashion in *The Washington Post* (March 6, 1963): "Harkins said the guerrillas obviously [!] are not being reinforced or supplied systematically from North Vietnam, China or any place. He said they apparently depend for weapons primarily upon whatever they can capture. Many of their weapons, he said, are homemade."*

That the basic sources of supply for the NLF remain the territory of South Vietnam and U.S. shipments is confirmed in two very recent unimpeachable sources. Max Frankel, from Washington, states in the *New York Times,* March 3, 1966, that it is thought the NLF may be receiving "an average daily flow of 12 to 30 tons of supplies from North Vietnam." He goes on, however, to state that probably 12 tons per day is the total need in terms of supply requirement and that: "The guerrillas try to live from the land in South Vietnam and make use of captured weapons and equipment." The meaning of this is clearer when it is observed, as Mr. Frankel states: "The United States is moving an average of 24,000 tons of supplies each day by ship alone plus an undisclosed amount by air."

Professor Bernard B. Fall, in the *New York Review* (March 17, 1966), agrees with and cites the statement in the *Times* of February 17, 1966, that about 40 per cent of all civilian goods "reach the Vietcong *directly* from the American ware-

* Senator Stephen Young of Ohio, having been in Southeast Asia in September and October 1965, said on the Senate floor, Jan. 20, 1966: "The fact is that the conflict raging in Vietnam is a civil war. General Westmoreland stated to me that the bulk of the Vietcong fighting in South Vietnam were born and reared in South Vietnam. General Stilwell, in Thailand, went further. He stated that 80 percent of the Vietcong fighting in the Mekong Delta area south of Saigon, were born and reared in that area. They were not infiltrators or Communists from the North."

houses" (italics in original). Professor Fall concludes that the emphasis upon supplies from North Vietnam is highly dubious and "that the enormous bombing effort in the North is even less effective than the more skeptical officers had predicted."

The U.S. government talks much now of the alleged presence of troops from the DRV in South Vietnam; its highly ambiguous reports give the impression that somewhere between ten thousand or twenty thousand such troops are in South Vietnam. In this connection note is to be taken first of the unequivocal statements made to us when in the DRV by the highest authorities—including the Prime Minister—that this assertion was the "sheerest fabrication." Second is to be noted the highly circumstantial and confusing character of the reports which do appear in the United States; and third the fact that contact with such troops always is "about" to take place but somehow never does. Since the war hawks like Secretary McNamara now claim DRV troop intervention goes back several years, attention should be called to the statement by David Halberstam in the *Times* (March 6, 1964): "No capture of North Vietnamese in the South has come to light."

If and when the NLF calls for help from the DRV in the form of troops such help will be forthcoming. But, in any case, to compare the presence of Vietnamese in Vietnam—and North Vietnam differs from South Vietnam very much less than Maine differs from Florida—with the presence of U.S. troops to the tune of a quarter of a million in Vietnam again is possible only in the face of a general irrationality that has descended upon the Administration forces.

Anti-Communism

Finally, within the arsenal of the Administration's argumentation are the trump cards of anti-Communism and negotiation from strength. Let us briefly deal with these.

86

In the Fall of 1963 the distinguished Professor Derk Bodde of the University of Pennsylvania cried out against the atrocities and tortures that besmirched the U.S.-backed war in Vietnam. He wrote:

"The excuse of Germans under Hitler was that they did not know what was happening, and could not have prevented it if they did. We as responsible citizens living in a democracy cannot use this excuse. When will we raise the voice of humanity and justice to say: 'This is immoral. It must stop?' " (*New York Times*, September 16, 1963.)

Professor Bodde noted that the excuse of the German population most commonly offered was ignorance. This is accurate; yet, at best, it must be recognized as largely flimsy. Certainly, the responsible figures in the government and in industry, finance and the armed forces—who administered and profited and enforced—knew well what was being done. They not only knew what they were doing but they boasted of it—*and they justified it*. And *their justification was anti-Communism*.

Their anti-Communism was in fact anti-humanism. They detested Marxism and saw in it kinship with liberalism, with democratic yearnings, with humanistic feelings, with scientific commitment. Hence, their anti-Communism—as the facade for a policy of super-exploitation and world conquest—was their essential instrument of progaganda; on that basis the German people were gulled and on that basis capitalist presses and governments throughout the world supported Hitler, forgave him everything and built him up until—as an implacable monster —he finally threatened their own systems and possessions.

When Hitler ordered the invasion of the USSR, he justified it this way, on June 22, 1941: "The Jewish-Bolshevik rulers alone have endeavored, from Moscow during the past two decades, to set on fire not only Germany, but the whole of Europe." Is that not Nixon's "twenty years of treason"? Is that not the core of McCarthyism? Is that not the point of the McCarran Act's preamble?

Says a recent study of nazi propaganda: "In the last years of the decade Nazi agitation against *Gesamtmarxismus,* and Communism in particular, was intensified until in 1932 *it culminated in the creation of an anti-Communist psychosis in Germany.*" (Z. A. B. Zeman, *Nazi Propaganda,* 1964, Oxford Univ. Press, p. 86; italics added.)

This, the author adds and the world knows, "was highly rewarding"; in 1933 the entire ultra-Right in Germany and "the industrialists, and the military, handed power over to Hitler because they believed that he would save the country from Communism."

Said the *Berliner Börsen-Zeitung*—the German equivalent of the *Wall Street Journal*—on November 10, 1935: "the forces of defense against the imperialist claims to power of the Third International are rallying. The struggle against the Comintern as the Bolshevik center of subversion and murder has to summon all the forces that do not want to see their nations and states sold out to Communist chaos. The aim is a broad front against international Communism."

Can anything be more familiar to present-day American readers? Is not the above, tomorrow's editorial in the New York *Daily News* and the St. Louis *Globe-Democrat* and the Oakland *Tribune* and—God help us—tomorrow's speeches from the President and the Vice-President?

Positions of Strength

When the American people—or the Senate Foreign Relations Committee, for that matter—are told anything these days from the White House, they learn that the Administration is strafing and bombing and burning because it really wants peace but it wants to negotiate for peace from a position of strength. Quite apart from the spectacle this presents of "democracy" in action, of an Alice-in-Wonderland description of peace-seeking conduct, it is vital to remember that the whole rationale is the alleged need to "negotiate from strength."

This is offered as something new; it is not new at all, however, but rather has characterized U.S. foreign policy generally since Truman. Defense Secretary McNamara in 1962 said: "Unless we are prepared to place everything at risk, we cannot hope to save anything from disaster." This is, of course, Dulles' "brinkmanship." McNamara now reiterates a military policy which is in fact Dulles' "massive retaliation" policy; when and if this is implemented, Hanson Baldwin reported (*New York Times,* February 27, 1965), the Pentagon pundits estimate that the United States will suffer about 125 million dead—but will be able to "win"!

To call this criminal insanity is simply to reveal the inadequacy of language devised prior to thermonuclear weapons. That in the face of this, people like Baldwin himself, and Max Ascoli and William V. Shannon—not to mention the *National Review* gang—have reconciled themselves to the "necessity" of war upon China and "to using what it takes to win" (the words are those of Baldwin in the *Times,* February 21, 1965) —reflects the contagious quality of this criminal insanity, when induced by a long-enough sustained campaign of anti-Communism.

There exists one careful, thorough and quite cool study of the U.S. post-war *tactic* of diplomacy. It was produced by an Australian scholar as a doctoral dissertation for the University of London and has been published in New York by Knopf (1963). This is Coral Bell's *Negotiation from Strength: A Study in the Politics of Power.* Professor Bell notes: "Ten years of negotiating from strength produced by 1960 an actual negotiating position much inferior to that of 1950." Her conclusions are pertinent to today's headlines: "in a period when the dangers attending diplomatic negotiations have been constantly stressed, it may be useful to point out that delay is not enough, that the process of postponing settlement is a process of reduction of choices. *To stand firm may be an admirable policy, but not if one happens to be standing in a patch of quicksand."* (Italics added.)

There is no better simile for U.S. military involvement in the vastnesses of Asia than to be caught standing in a patch of quicksand and the longer we remain and the more frantically we thrash about the deeper does the United States sink. What is projected with the continuance of the present disaster course is already beginning to appear in "trial balloons." Thus, Seymour Topping, writing from Saigon (*New York Times,* February 26, 1966), says that there "official planning no longer takes account of any possibility of peace negotiations" with the NLF and that the future seems to be one of perhaps seven years of intensive war, with casualties among U.S. troops amounting to about 9,000 per month—i.e., a total of about 750,000 American troops killed and wounded! And those advocating this course are the "patriots"! Furthermore, no one can get from these "patriots" just what they see as "victory" after these seven years of slaughter—and how or why the killing should then really terminate.

Are the Revolutionary Vietnamese Pawns?

Those who, in Pentagon circles hope and in some peace and Left groupings fear, that the Vietnamese people are to be mere pawns within the grinding power of egocentric Great Powers are making a serious mistake.

90

Certainly all powers—great and not-so-great—have national interests and all governments try to serve those interests—*as they see them*. But those governments which serve monopoly capitalist economies and those that serve socialist economies have basically different orientations and therefore fundamentally divergent definitions of "national interest."

Monopoly powers regret the termination of colonialism; to the degree that their remaining strength permits they seek in all possible ways to preserve colonialism knowing that it has bulwarked them in the past and serves them in the present. Socialist powers on the other hand have basic interests that are anti-colonial and no significant interests that favor the retention of that system; they will, therefore, throw their weight on the side of the forces of national liberation.

Specifically, the peoples in Indo-China rebelled against French rule incessantly but without success throughout the century-long travail of that rule. It was only with World War II and its conclusion that their revolutionary effort could succeed. This was not because their leaders had suddenly become more brave or more clever; it is because the relationship of forces in the world—and in Asia—had decisively shifted away from imperialism and toward socialism and anti-colonialism.

In generations gone by, a few gun-boats and a few regiments were sufficient to suppress the most serious uprisings of the Vietnamese people. In our time, a major commitment by France reinforced by arms and billions from the United States failed to suppress the national-liberation movement. And today, every weapon in the arsenal of the United States—except one—has been hurled upon the Vietnamese and they stand erect and undefeated.

This is owing in the first place to their own valor and morale and ingenuity; but all these together would not suffice, as the

Vietnamese themselves are the first to emphasize, if there were not also in the world 14 socialist nations and if their materiel, diplomatic, and economic help were not present. Should the Vietnamese government and people ask for more direct assistance—including troops, planes and ships—these will be forthcoming in any quantity necessary; but they will not be forthcoming until the NLF and/or the DRV request such help.

The Way Out is Out

Lately, the opposition to Administration policy has reached such vast and deafening proportions that even President Johnson has deigned to admit the existence of something less than a "consensus" behind it. But the President has chosen to dismiss the significance of the dissenters; he says they are "merely worriers" and that they do not present a real alternative to his own course.

I do not feel ashamed to confess to being worried about the Administration's policy, but I insist that the dissenters do have a perfectly reasonable, practical and honorable alternative to the dominant Washington course. And it is the Geneva Agreement of 1954.

The United States must do in Vietnam what the French did in Vietnam—and in Algeria. The United States must disengage itself from that area and must withdraw its forces. France having done this, did the prestige, the influence or the honor of that country diminish therefor? Is not the contrary true?

The United States must cease the bombing of North Vietnam unconditionally, permanently and at once. It must agree to a cease-fire; it must announce its firm decision to honor and implement the Geneva Agreement; it must face the fact that the National Liberation Front exists, is indigenous and does in fact represent—as all competent witnesses have testified for years—the overwhelming majority of the population of South Vietnam.

Geneva must be reconvened and this must be done not under the auspices of the United Nations—in which neither Hanoi nor Peking nor Saigon nor the NLF is represented!—but under the auspices of the International Commission established by Geneva. Confirming the recognition of the unity, integrity and sovereignty of Vietnam, beginning the process of the withdrawal of troops from that country, and welcoming a prolonged process for the peaceful reunification of the country to culminate in a general and free election, under the aegis of the Geneva machinery—there is a realistic, practical and necessary alternative to the present cruel and suicidal course of the Johnson Administration.

Let no one despair of its accomplishment. Some—moved by ultra-Leftist views—assert that "it is not possible to alter the foreign policy of a capitalist nation." This is absurd; such alteration has occurred regularly in the past—for the better and for the worse. Was the foreign policy of Churchill the same as that of Chamberlain? Were they not both Tories, and surely neither favored socialism! But one was a chief architect of Munich and the other hated Munich. "Small" difference; merely a tactical collision! Merely, indeed!

Was FDR's foreign policy that of Herbert Hoover? Of course both were partisans of capitalism but one viewed Latin America in the traditional "dollar diplomacy" way and the other did not; one refused to recognize the existence of the Soviet Union and the other did recognize it; one was so obsessed with anti-Communist poison that he would have preferred anything—Hitler included—to any kind of collaboration with the Soviet Union and the other saw fundamental distinctions between fascism and socialism and envisaged, in his last months, the possibility of a friendship between the USA and the USSR persisting after the comradeship of war.

There is good evidence that the outlook of Kennedy in the final months of his life was considerably different from what it had been when he took office and certainly was different from the outlook dominating Eisenhower's Administration.

Again, forces outside the United States and forces inside the United States can induce significant changes in American foreign policy.

Some tend to despair because they do not see the "effects" though the efforts have been considerable. But, of course, one sees the effects when they appear and not before; and when they do appear it is as a result of enormous efforts. Certain it is that in mid-1965 only two Senators articulated their opposition to Administration foreign policy and now 50—half the Senate—have expressed their doubts or their antagonism. Similar developments have appeared in the House and qualified correspondents state that:

"Rarely have Americans been so uneasy. Rarely have they been stricken by quite such a crisis of conscience. Rarely have they been so obsessed with a single subject: Vietnam.

"I was in Washington the other day. The mood there was dark. . . . The Vietnam war has everybody in its grip. Everybody wants to escape." (Erwin D. Canham, *Christian Science Monitor,* February 19, 1966.)

And T.R.B. from Washington: "We do not recall ever having seen such a change of sentiment in six months as we sense here in Washington about this war. Of course we could be mistaken. We don't think so. The uneasiness and doubts are widely expressed." (*New Republic,* March 5, 1966.)

Now the opposition has reached such bodies as SNCC, the

94

American Jewish Congress and the Amalgamated Clothing Workers of America (AFL-CIO), with its 400,000 members. Meanwhile the antagonism on the campuses, within the intellectual community as a whole, and among religious and women's organizations and civil rights fighters not only has not abated; it actually has intensified.

The progress in the movement for peace has been fantastic. This is cause for renewed and invigorated confidence and not despair. Given the present momentum I think it is not quixotic to project a demonstration for peace in the city of Washington numbering one million Americans; just imagine what that would mean—*one million Americans* coming to Washington— perhaps just before the November elections of 1966!—and demanding an end to the killing in Vietnam.

Never since the days of chattel slavery has a question of right and wrong been clearer in the United States than it is today with the war in Vietnam. Among those who opposed slavery there were many differences, but finally one thing united them all: a sense of humanity, of decency, a concern for fundamental morality.

The differences that seemed so important to the various groups in the anti-slavery effort now have interest only to historians; but the greatest lesson they can teach us today is this: Whatever prevented unity in the struggle against slavery was helpful to the slaveowners. Whatever prevents unity now in the struggle to *stop the killing in Vietnam* is helpful only to the "crack-pot realists" and the "stone-age" generals.

We must go to the American people in their multi-millions and say to them confidently, plainly and convincingly—in terms that they understand and can move them—that this war is atrocious, immoral, and intensely harmful to our country and to our own everyday interests.

We must not admit even the possibility of failure in this great crusade. We will not fail. We will succeed and that success will be an indispensable part of the process of making our nation a beacon of decency, justice, equality and peace.

PART THREE

Documentary Supplement

I.

THE GENEVA AGREEMENTS, 1954

A. AGREEMENT ON THE CESSATION OF HOSTILITIES IN VIETNAM
(July 20, 1954)

(Signed on behalf of the Commander-in-Chief of French Union Forces in Indochina and Commander-in-Chief of the People's Army of Vietnam.)

I. "A *provisional military demarcation line* shall be fixed, on either side of which the forces of the two parties shall be regrouped after their withdrawal, the forces of the People's Army of Vietnam to the north of the line and the forces of the French Union to the south. . . .

II. "The period within which the movement of all forces of either party into its regrouping zone on either side of the *provisional military demarcation line* shall not exceed three hundred days. . . .

XVI. ". . . the introduction into Vietnam of any troop reinforcements and additional military personnel is prohibited. . . .

XVII. ". . . the introduction into Vietnam of any reinforcements in the form of all types of arms, munitions and other war matériel . . . is prohibited. . . .

XVIII. ". . . the establishment of new military bases is prohibited through Vietnam territory. . . .

XIX. ". . . no military base under the control of a foreign State may be established in the regrouping zone of either party; the two parties shall ensure that the zones assigned to them do not adhere to any military alliance and are not used for the resumption of hostilities or to further an aggressive policy. . . ."

B. FINAL DECLARATION
*Geneva Conference (July 21, 1954)**

1. "The Conference takes note of the agreements ending hostilities. . . .

2. ". . . will permit Cambodia, Laos, and Vietnam henceforth to play their part, in full independence and sovereignty, in the peaceful community of nations. . . .

4. ". . . prohibiting the introduction into Vietnam of foreign troops and military personnel as well as of all kinds of arms and munitions. . . .

5. ". . . no military base under the control of a foreign state may be established in the regrouping zones of the two parties. . . .

6. "The Conference recognizes that the essential purpose of the agreement relating to Vietnam is to settle military questions with a view to ending hostilities and that the military demarcation line is provisional and should not in any way be interpreted as constituting a political or territorial boundary. . . .

7. "The Conference declares that, so far as Vietnam is concerned, the settlement of political problems, effected on the basis of respect for the principles of independence, unity, and territorial integrity, shall permit the Vietnamese people to enjoy the fundamental freedoms, guaranteed by democratic institutions established as a result of free general elections by secret ballot. In order to ensure that sufficient progress in the restoration of peace has been made, and that all the necessary conditions obtain for free expression of the national will, general elections shall be held in July, 1956, under the supervision of an international commission composed of representatives of the Member States of the International Supervisory Commission. . . .

11. ". . . the French Government will proceed from the principle of respect for the independence and sovereignty, unity, and territorial integrity of Cambodia, Laos, and Vietnam

12. "In their relations with Cambodia, Laos, and Vietnam, each member of the Geneva Conference undertakes to respect the sovereignty, the independence, the unity, and the territorial integrity of the above-mentioned States, and to refrain from any interference in their internal affairs."

* Participating were: Cambodia, Democratic Republic of Vietnam, France, Laos, People's Republic of China, State of Vietnam, USSR, Great Britain, USA. This Declaration was approved by voice vote of all above States.

II.

THE PROGRAM OF THE SOUTH VIETNAM NATIONAL LIBERATION FRONT (NLF)

(Announced, December 20, 1960)

Since the French colonialists invaded their country, all the Vietnamese people have unremittingly struggled for national independence and freedom. In 1945, our compatriots throughout the country rose up, overthrew the Japanese and French domination and seized power, and afterwards heroically carried out a resistance war for nine years, defeated the French aggressors and the U.S. interventionists, and brought our people's valiant resistance war to glorious victory.

At the July 1954 Geneva Conference, the French imperialists had to undertake to withdraw their troops from Vietnam. The countries participating in the Conference solemnly declared their recognition of the sovereignty, independence, unity and territorial integrity of Vietnam.

Since then we should have been able to enjoy peace, and join with the people throughout the country in building an independent, democratic, unified, prosperous and strong Vietnam.

However, the American imperialists, who had in the past helped the French colonialists to massacre our people, have plotted to perpetuate the partition of our country, enslave its southern part through a disguised colonial regime and turn it into a military base in preparation for aggressive war in Southeast Asia. They have brought their puppets, the Ngo Dinh Diem* clique, to power under a signboard of fake independence, and use their "aid" policy and advisers' machine to keep tight control over all military, economic, political and cultural branches in South Vietnam.

The aggressors and the traitors have set up the most dictatorial and cruel rule ever seen in Vietnam's history. They repress and persecute all democratic and patriotic movements, abolish all human liberties. They monopolize all branches of economy, strangle industry,

---

* Ngo Dinh Diem, put in power by the United States, ruled South Vietnam from 1954 to November 1963, when he was assassinated, together with his brother Nhu, during the generals' coup. Since then, although there have been many changes in the Saigon regime, the nature of the government has not changed.

agriculture and trade, ruthlessly exploit all strata of the people. They use every device of mind-poisoning, obscurantism and deprivation in an attempt to quell the patriotism of our people. They feverishly increase their military forces, build military bases, use the army as a tool for repression of the people and war preparation in accordance with the U.S. imperialists' policy.

For more than six years, countless crimes have been perpetrated by the U.S.-Diem dictatorial and cruel regime: the sound of gunfire has never ceased throughout South Vietnam; tens of thousands of patriots have been shot dead, beheaded or disembowelled with their livers plucked out; hundreds of thousands of people have been tortured and thrown into jail where they have slowly perished; countless people have been the victims of arson, forcible removal from their homes and usurpation of land, and impressed for forced labor or into the army; countless families are disrupted as a result of the policy of concentrating people in "prosperity zones" and "agricultural settlements"; exorbitant rents and taxes, terror, arrests, plunder, extortion and widespread unemployment and poverty are seriously threatening the lives of all strata of the people.

Peace! Independence! Democracy! Enough food and clothing! Peaceful reunification of the Fatherland!

Those are our most earnest and pressing aspirations. They have crystallized into an iron will, and a prodigious force urging our people to unite and resolutely rise up to overthrow the cruel rule of the U.S. imperialists and their puppets, for national salvation.

To serve the supreme interests of the Fatherland, and struggle to the end for the people's legitimate aspirations, the South Vietnam National Liberation Front has come into being, in full accordance with the progressive trend in the world.

The South Vietnam National Liberation Front undertakes to unite people of all walks of life, all social classes, nationalities, political parties, organizations, religious communities, and all patriotic personalities in South Vietnam, without distinction of political tendency, in order to struggle to overthrow the rule of the U.S. imperialists and their henchmen in South Vietnam and realize independence, improvement of living conditions, peace and neutrality in South Vietnam, and advance towards peaceful reunification of the Fatherland.

The program of the South Vietnam National Liberation Front includes the following ten points:

100

I. Overthrow the disguised colonial regime of the U.S. imperialists and the dictatorial Ngo Dinh Diem administration—lackey of the USA—and form a national democratic coalition government.

The present regime in South Vietnam is a disguised colonial regime set up by the U.S. imperialists. The South Vietnam administration is a lackey which has been carrying out the U.S. imperialists' political line. This regime and administration must be overthrown and a broad national democratic coalition government formed, including representatives of all strata of the people, of all nationalities, political parties, and religious communities, and of patriotic personalities. We must wrest back the people's economic, political, social and cultural rights, realize independence and democracy, improve the people's living conditions, carry out a policy of peace and neutrality and advance toward peaceful reunification of the Fatherland.

II. Bring into being a broad and progressive democracy.

1. Abolish the current constitution of the Ngo Dinh Diem dictatorial administration—lackey of the United States. Elect a new National Assembly through universal suffrage.

2. Promulgate all democratic freedoms: freedom of expression, of the press, of assembly, of association, of trade unions, of movements. Guarantee freedom of belief; no discrimination on the part of the State against any religion. Grant freedom of action to all patriotic political parties and mass organizations, irrespective of political tendency.

3. Grant general amnesty to all political detainees, dissolve all concentration camps under any form whatsoever. Abolish the fascist law 10-59* and other anti-democratic laws. Permit the return of all those who had to flee abroad due to the U.S.-Diem regime.

4. Strictly ban all illegal arrests and imprisonments, tortures and corporal punishment. Punish unrepentant murderers of the people.

III. Build an independent and sovereign economy, improve the people's living conditions.

1. Abolish the economic monopoly of the U.S. imperialists and their henchmen. Build an independent and sovereign economy and finance, beneficial to the nation and people. Confiscate and nationalize

---

* Enacted in 1959, this notorious law set life imprisonment or the death penalty for anyone "committing a crime against the security of the state or harboring an intent to commit such a crime."

all property of the U.S. imperialists and the ruling clique, their puppets.

2. Help industrialists and tradespeople rehabilitate and develop industry large and small, and encourage industrial development. Actively protect home-produced goods by abolishing production taxes, restricting or ending the import of goods which can be produced within the country and reducing import taxes on raw materials and machinery.

3. Rehabilitate agriculture, and modernize farming, fishing and animal husbandry. Help peasants reclaim waste land and develop production; protect crops and ensure outlets for agricultural products.

4. Encourage and accelerate the economic interflow between town and countryside, and between the plain and mountain areas. Develop trade with foreign countries without distinction of political regime, and on the principle of equality and mutual benefit.

5. Apply an equitable and rational tax system. Abolish arbitrary fines.

6. Promulgate labor regulations, prohibit dismissals, wage cuts, fines and ill-treatment of workers and employees, improve the life of workers and public employees, and fix wages and guarantee health protection for young apprentices.

7. Organize social security:

—Jobs for the unemployed.

—Protection of orphans, and of the aged and disabled.

—Assistance to those who have become disabled or are without support as a result of their struggle against U.S. imperialism and its puppets.

—Relief to localities suffering crop failures, fire and natural calamities.

8. Help displaced persons return to their native places if they so desire, and provide jobs for those who decide to remain in the South.

9. Strictly prohibit forcible removals of people from their homes, arson, usurpation of land, and herding of people into concentration centers. Ensure to the country folk and urban working people the opportunity to earn their living in security.

IV. Carry out land rent reduction and advance toward the settlement of the agrarian problem so as to ensure land to the tillers.

1. Carry out land rent reduction. Guarantee the peasants' right to till their present plots of land and ensure the right of ownership for those who have reclaimed waste land. Protect the peasants'

legitimate right of ownership on the plots of land distributed to them.

2. Abolish all "prosperity zones" and prohibit the herding of people into "agricultural settlements." Permit those forcibly herded into "prosperity zones" or "agricultural settlements" to return home freely and earn their living on their own plots of land.

3. Confiscate the land usurped by the U.S. imperialists and their agents, and distribute it to landless and land-poor peasants. Redistribute communal land in an equitable and rational way.

4. Through negotiations, the State will purchase from landowners at equitable and rational prices all land held by them in excess of a given area to be fixed in accordance with the concrete situation in each locality, and distribute it to landless and land-poor peasants. This land will be distributed free of charge and with no conditions attached.

V. Build a national and democratic education and culture.

1. Eliminate the servile and corrupt American-style culture and education; build a national, progressive culture and education serving the Fatherland and the people.

2. Wipe out illiteracy. Build general education schools in sufficient number for the youth and children. Expand universities and vocational and professional schools. Use the Vietnamese language at all levels of education. Reduce school fees; exempt poor pupils and students from paying fees; reform the examination system.

3. Develop science and technology and national literature and art; encourage and help intellectuals, and cultural and art workers to develop their abilities in the service of national construction.

4. Develop medical services to protect the people's health. Expand the physical culture and sports movement.

VI. Build an army to defend the Fatherland and the people.

1. Build a national army to defend the Fatherland and the people. Abolish the system of U.S. military advisers.

2. Abolish press-ganging. Improve the material life of the army men and ensure their political rights. Prohibit the ill-treatment of soldiers. Apply a policy of assistance to families of poor army men.

3. Give rewards and worthy jobs to all officers and soldiers who have rendered meritorious services in the struggle against the domination of the U.S. imperialists and their henchmen. Observe leniency toward those who had collaborated with the U.S.-Diem clique and

committed crimes against the people but have later repented and served the people.

4. Abolish all foreign military bases in South Vietnam.

VII. Guarantee equality among the various nationalities, and between men and women; protect the legitimate rights of foreign residents in Vietnam and Vietnamese living abroad.

1. Ensure the right of autonomy to all national minorities. Set up, within the framework of the great family of the Vietnamese people, autonomous regions in areas inhabited by minority people.

Ensure equal rights among different nationalities. All nationalities have the right to use and develop their own spoken and written languages and to preserve or change their customs and habits. Abolish the U.S.-Diem clique's present policy of ill-treatment and forced assimilation of the minority nationalities.

Help the minority peoples catch up with the general level by developing economy and culture in areas inhabited by them and by training skilled personnel from people of minority origin.

2. Ensure equality between men and women. Women shall enjoy the same rights as men in all fields: political, economic, cultural and social.

3. Protect the legitimate rights of foreigners residing in Vietnam.

4. Defend and take care of the interests of Vietnamese living abroad.

VIII. Carry out a foreign policy of peace and neutrality.

1. Cancel all unequal treaties signed with foreign countries by the U.S. henchmen, which violate national sovereignty.

2. Establish diplomatic relations with all countries irrespective of political regime, in accordance with the principles of peaceful coexistence as put forth at the Bandung Conference.

3. Unite closely with the peace-loving and neutral countries. Expand friendly relations with Asian and African countries, first of all, with neighboring Cambodia and Laos.

4. Refrain from joining any bloc or military alliance or forming a military alliance with any country.

5. Accept economic aid from any country ready to assist Vietnam without conditions attached.

IX. Re-establish normal relations between the two zones and advance toward peaceful reunification of the Fatherland.

The urgent demand of our people throughout the country is to reunify the Fatherland by peaceful means. The South Vietnam National Liberation Front advocates the gradual reunification of the country by peaceful means, through negotiations and discussions between the two zones on all forms and measures beneficial to the Vietnamese people and Fatherland.

Pending national reunification, the governments of the two zones will negotiate and undertake not to use any propaganda likely to sow division among the people or to kindle war, nor to use military forces against each other. Carry out economic and cultural exchanges between the two zones. Ensure for the people of both zones freedom of movement and trade, and the right to exchange visits and correspondence.

X. Oppose aggressive war, actively defend world peace.

1. Oppose aggressive war and all forms of enslavement by the imperialists. Support the national liberation struggles of the peoples of other countries.

2. Oppose war propaganda. Demand general disarmament, prohibition of nuclear weapons, and the use of atomic energy for peaceful purposes.

3. Support the movements for peace, democracy and social progress in the world. Actively contribute to the safeguarding of peace in South-East Asia and the world.

Compatriots throughout the country!
All Vietnamese patriots!

Following nearly a century of struggle and nine years of resistance, our people, who have shed so much of their blood, are determined not to be enslaved again!

For the peace, independence, freedom and reunification of our Fatherland, for the destiny of our people, for the sake of our own lives and future and the future of our descendants,

Let all of us rise up! Let all of us unite!

Let us close our ranks and march forward under the banner of the South Vietnam National Liberation Front to overthrow the cruel domination of the U.S. imperialists and the Ngo Dinh Diem clique, their henchmen, in order to save the country and our homes.

We shall surely win, because the union of our people is an invincible force, because justice belongs to us and because colonialism is an anachronism in full decay and is heading for total collapse. In the world, the movement for peace, democracy and national independence is expanding in breadth and strength and is winning more and more successes. This situation is very favorable to our struggle for national liberation.

The U.S. imperialists and their henchmen are doomed to failure!

The struggle for national liberation in South Vietnam will certainly be victorious!

Let us unite, be confident and struggle valiantly!

Forward to a glorious victory for our people and our Fatherland!

III.

THE LEADERSHIP OF THE SOUTH VIETNAM NATIONAL LIBERATION FRONT

Some idea of the breadth of the NLF may be obtained by examining the personalities in its leadership. The Commission for Foreign Relations of the NLF, which supplied the list that follows, adds: "The specific conditions of our fight impose certain restrictions so that for the time being we cannot include some of our outstanding leaders and delegates, especially those men and women who are struggling in areas still controlled by the enemy." With these exceptions, then, here is the leadership of the NLF:

(1) NGUYEN HUU THO, *President, Presidium, Central Committee.* Born in 1910 in Cholon, South Vietnam; his family was in good circumstances. He studied law in Paris and served as an attorney for many years in Saigon; he was especially known as a civil liberties attorney, defending many celebrated cases challenging French colonial rule. As a leader of students, faculty members and other intelligentsia he was jailed in 1950; after a brief period of freedom—and struggle—following the Geneva Agreement in 1954, he again was arrested and spent several years in various prisons. In 1961 he escaped confinement and since that time he has held the above-mentioned post.

(2) YBIH ALEO, *Vice-President, Presidium, Central Committee.* Born in 1901 in the hamlet of Nieng, in central Vietnam. He is of the Edeh national minority and is a Protestant in religion. During his youth, while in the French colonial army, he participated in revolutionary activity and was a leader in the 1945 national uprising against

106

colonial rule. He was arrested in 1946 and sentenced to death; this was later changed to life imprisonment. He was released finally in 1951 and in the late 1950's became one of the leaders in the struggle against the Diem-U.S. forces.

(3) Vo Chi Cong, *Vice-President, Presidium, Central Committee.* Born in 1912 in central Vietnam. By the age of 16 he was active in revolutionary struggles and throughout the 1930's was a leader therein. In 1941 he was sentenced to life imprisonment but the 1945 uprising liberated him. Since then he has played a leading role in revolutionary struggle.

(4) Dr. Phung Van Cung, *Vice-President, Presidium, Central Committee.* Born in 1909 in the South. His medical education was completed at Hanoi and he was an outstanding physician and hospital administrator; during this experience he persisted in underground revolutionary work and finally left for the liberated areas in 1960.

(5) Thom Me The Nhem, *Vice-President, Presidium, Central Committee.* Born in 1912 in the South; he is of Khmer nationality and has been a Buddhist monk since childhood. As a leading Buddhist he opposed French colonial rule and continued his struggle against religious and national oppression that followed the repudiation of Geneva and especially the fierce Diem repressions.

(6) Huynh Tan Phat, *Vice-President, Presidium, Central Committee.* Born in the South in 1913 and is a well-known architect. In the 1930's he was editor of a militant youth magazine and a leader of the "Vanguard Youth" movement. He was twice arrested by the French colonialists; he was in charge of the Information Service for South Vietnam during the war against the French and after Geneva continued the struggle for independence; he moved to the liberated areas in 1958. He is General Secretary of the Democratic Party of South Vietnam.

(7) Tran Nam Trung, *Vice-President, Presidium, Central Committee.* Born in a peasant family in central Vietnam in 1913. He participated in revolutionary struggles from a very early age and was jailed many times.

(8) Mme. Nguyen Thi Dinh, *Member, Presidium, Central Committee.* Born in a peasant family in South Vietnam in 1920. She participated in revolutionary struggles as a girl and was jailed in 1939; she remained in prison until freed by the 1945 Revolution. She was an outstanding leader in the struggle against the French until victory

in 1954 and is now Chairman of the South Vietnam Women's Union for Liberation and is Deputy-Commander of the Armed Forces of the NLF.

(9) THICH THIEN HAO, *Member, Presidium, Central Committee.* Born of peasant stock in South Vietnam in 1909. As President of the Vietnam Luc Hoa Buddhists' Association he was an outstanding opponent of the religious persecution policies of the Saigon regimes after Geneva.

(10) TRAN BUU KIEM, *Member, Presidium, Central Committee.* Born in South Vietnam in 1921; he is an attorney, having graduated from the Faculty of Law at Hanoi University. He was a leader of the General Association of Indo-Chinese Students in the struggle against the French prior to 1945, and in the war from 1946 to 1954 held responsible positions in the revolutionary effort in the South.

(11) NGUYEN VAN NGOI, *Member, Presidium, Central Committee.* His Eminence Superior Nguyen Van Ngoi was born in South Vietnam in 1900 and was a school superintendent for some time. Converted to the Cao Dai religion in 1927, he headed the Cao Dai Committee for National Salvation during the Resistance War. He is President of the Tien Thien Cao Dai sect and joined the liberated areas in 1960.

(12) LE VAN HUAN, *Assistant Secretary-General, Central Committee.* Born of peasant stock in South Vietnam in 1906. For many years he was a high-school teacher; in 1954 he was a founder of the Saigon-Cholon Peace Movement. He was jailed in 1955 and spent five years in various prisons. In 1960 was sent to the liberated areas.

(13) HO THU, *Assistant General-Secretary, Central Committee.* Born into a mandarin family in central Vietnam in 1910, educated in Paris as a pharmacist, has participated in revolutionary struggles from his youth. He fought in the Resistance War from 1951 to 1954; after Geneva he was arrested. After six years in various prisons, he escaped and has been in the liberated area since 1961.

(14) UNG NGOC KY, *Member, Secretariat, Central Committee.* Born in South Vietnam in 1920; he was a leading intellectual in the anti-French resistance in Saigon and during the War of Resistance edited the newspaper, *Doc Lap* (Independence), organ of the Democratic Party. He is now assistant secretary-general of the Democratic Party in South Vietnam.

(15) LE VAN THINH, *Member, Central Committee.* Born in North Vietnam in 1920 and participated in revolutionary struggles as a

108

mere boy. He was jailed in the notorious Poulo Condor prison under the French and liberated after the 1945 Revolution; thereafter he fought in the Resistance in South Vietnam. In 1962 he was appointed Head of the Permanent Mission of the NLF in Cuba.

(16) TRAN VAN THANH, *Member, Central Committee.* Born in South Vietnam in 1921, he joined the revolutionary movement at a very young age. He was held prisoner in Poulo Condor for years and was liberated in the 1945 Revolution. Following Geneva, he was a leading figure in trade union efforts in the Saigon area; in 1960 he went to the liberated areas and since 1964, he has headed the NLF Mission in Peking.

(17) NGUYEN VAN HIEU, *Member, Central Committee.* Born in South Vietnam in 1922, Mr. Nguyen Van Hieu, under the pen-name, Khai Minh, was one of the best known authors and intellectuals in Saigon. He opposed the Diem clique and finally was forced to move into liberated areas in 1958. He is now head of the NLF Mission in both Prague and Berlin.

(18) MME. NGUYEN THI BINH, *Member, Central Committee.* The grand-daughter of Phan Chu Trinh, a renowned patriot, she was born in Saigon in 1927. As a school girl she made her mark as a leader of various student and intellectual organizations; in 1950 she was the leader of the Progressive Women's Association. From 1951 until Geneva in 1954 she was in prison; after being freed she again threw herself into the effort for a united and democratic Vietnam. In the recent past she has headed several NLF delegations to international gatherings.

(19) JOSEPH MARIE HO HUE BA, *Member, Central Committee.* A Roman Catholic priest, born in 1898 in South Vietnam. Until 1945 he was a seminary teacher; thereafter as Vice-President of the Catholics' Association in Long Xuyen province he was an active Resistance member. Rejecting the betrayal of Geneva, he has been a leader in the NLF from its foundation.

(20) MME. LE THI RIENG, *Member, Central Committee.* Born in South Vietnam in 1925; she worked in a weaving mill and as a girl participated in the underground struggle against the French. In 1945 she was the leader of the Women's Union for National Salvation and ever since has continued her liberation efforts.

(21) THICH HUNG TU, *Member, Central Committee.* Born in central Vietnam in 1902; his family were peasants. He has been an

outstanding Buddhist leader for many years, becoming Superior Bonze in Phan Thiet in 1935. He has actively resisted French and Saigon persecutions of his religion and is now President of the Buddhists' Association in the eastern part of South Vietnam; as such he is a leader in the general liberation effort.

(22) LE VAN THA, *Member, Central Committee*. Born in South Vietnam in 1914; under the French he was a professor and electrical engineer. While studying in France he joined the Vietnamese liberation effort; expelled by the French, he was jailed in Saigon. Released after the 1954 Agreement, he was re-arrested within a year, and held in jail from 1955 until 1961; thereafter he entered the liberated areas. He is a leader of the Radical-Socialist Party of South Vietnam.

(23) DANG QUANG MINH, *Member, Central Committee*. Born in South Vietnam in 1909; as a teacher he entered the movement for national independence in 1927. He was jailed in 1930 and imprisoned for several years. Released, he returned to revolutionary work and was jailed in 1940, and this time sent to Poulo Condor prison. The success of the 1945 Revolution freed him. From 1945 to 1954 he played an outstanding role in the struggle against the French, and after Geneva was a leader in the peace movement in South Vietnam. In 1961 he went to the liberated areas; he is now head of the NLF Mission in Moscow.

(24) ROCHOM BRIU, of Jarai nationality, was born in the hamlet of Ama H'Bu, near Pleiku in 1922. The French authorities relieved him of his post as teacher in Pleiku because of his anti-colonial utterances; in 1945 he was elected to the Pleiku People's Council. Two years later the French arrested him, but he escaped from prison in 1949 and since then has been an outstanding liberation figure. He is Secretary-General of the Autonomous Nationalities' Movement.

(25) COLONEL VO VAN MON, *Member, Central Committee*. Born in South Vietnam in 1918; after Geneva, he was Commander-in-Chief of the Binh Xuyen troops which resisted the Diem-U.S. efforts at repression. With the creation of the NLF, he and all the Binh Xuyen forces under him, joined the Front.

(26) TRAN HOAI NAM, *Member, Central Committee*. Born in central Vietnam in 1922, he participated in the anti-colonial struggles from an early age. He was a trade union leader for several years and held responsible military posts during the 1945-54 War against the French.

(27) TRAN HUU TRANG, *Member, Central Committee*. Born in

110

South Vietnam in 1906. By the early 1930's, he had established himself as one of Vietnam's leading playwrights; throughout the 40's and 50's he was a leading figure and organizer among Saigon writers and theatrical workers and in 1960 left for the liberated areas.

(28) NGUYEN VAN TIEN, *Member, Central Committee*. A leading Vietnamese intellectual; born in South Vietnam in 1919; was a professor in several universities under the French and joined the resistance movement in 1945. He has been entrusted by the NLF with many missions abroad since 1962.

(29) NGUYEN NGOC THUONG, *Member, Central Committee*. Born in a well-off family in South Vietnam in 1923. He studied at universities in both Saigon and Hanoi, taught in various high schools, edited a review called *Justice* and participated in various anti-French struggles. After Geneva he was arrested several times and finally left in 1960 for the liberated areas. He is a leader of the Radical-Socialist Party of South Vietnam.

(30) VO DONG GIANG, *Member, Central Committee*. Born in a worker's family in South Vietnam in 1921 and from boyhood has participated in workers' and national liberation struggles. He has held responsible positions abroad for the NLF.

(31) HOANG BICH SON, *Member, Central Committee*. Born in 1924 in South Vietnam. He was a leader in student movements from a very early age and continued as such until 1960 when he left for the liberated areas. He has served the NLF in important foreign missions.

(32) MME. MA THI CHU, *Member, Central Committee*. Born in South Vietnam in 1924. She carried out underground activities during the Resistance War against the French. After 1954, in her post on the pharmaceutical faculty in Saigon University, she continued her efforts for independence. She was jailed by Diem and tortured. In 1961 she went to the liberated areas and is now a member of the NLF Mission in Prague.

(33) LE QUANG CHANH, *Member, Central Committee*. Born in South Vietnam in 1924 and by profession a teacher. He participated in the War against the French and from 1954 to 1961, was on the Executive Committee of the South Vietnam Liberation Youth Federation. Since 1963, he has headed the NLF Mission in Indonesia.

(34) HUYNH VAN TAM, *Member, Central Committee*. Born in Saigon in 1919 and led the resistance to the Japanese in that city. Thereafter he was a leader in resistance against the French and in

111

1960 came to the liberated areas. Since 1963 he has headed the NLF Mission in Algiers.

(35) MME. NGUYEN THI TU, *Vice-Chairman, Liberation Women's Union of South Vietnam.* Born in South Vietnam in 1923. She was a leader in a trade union of bakers and cooks in Saigon and of various women's organizations. She was jailed several times and served time in Poulo Condor. In 1961 she entered the liberated areas.

(36) MME. THANH LOAN, *Vice-President, Liberation Women's Union.* Born in 1927 in South Vietnam, she has been one of the best-known actresses of Vietnam. During the Resistance War she founded the Artists' Mutual Assistance Union and was a leader of the Trade Union of Saigon Actors and Stage Setters from 1955 on. In 1963 she went to the liberated areas.

(37) HUYNH THANH MUNG, *Major, NLF forces.* Born in 1919 in South Vietnam. He was an officer in the "French Union" forces during World War II, and a military instructor in the Cao Dai Holy See from 1945 to 1954. In 1957 at the order of the Cao Dai Pope he collaborated with the Diem-U.S. forces but soon broke with them and joined the liberation army—with his entire battalion—in 1960. He has been an outstanding military leader in the NLF ever since.

(38) MME. ROCHOM BAN, *Member, Autonomous Nationalities' Movement.* A Jarai national, born near Pleiku in 1943. She joined the struggle for national liberation as a girl and since 1955 has performed heroically on behalf of the forces of independence.

(39) MME. AMI DOAN, *Vice-President, Autonomous Nationalities' Movement.* Born in a hamlet in Darlak province (central Vietnam) in 1923; she is of Jarai nationality. She has been a leader and inspirational figure in the resistance and liberation movement for 20 years.

(40) CHAU HOANG NAM, *Political Leader, Ap Bac Battalion.* Born in South Vietnam in 1932. He joined the resistance forces at the age of 14 and has been in almost continuous combat since. He has been in over 100 engagements and has been wounded 11 times. He was in command at the time of the major victory by liberation forces at the Ap Bac battle early in 1963, and continues now in command of resistance troops.

IV.

THE "FOUR POINTS" OF THE DEMOCRATIC REPUBLIC OF VIETNAM

The "four points" of the DRV constitute an official summary of that government's position in terms of settling the war in Vietnam. They were stated in the Report made to the National Assembly of the DRV by Prime Minister Pham Van Dong, April 8, 1965; the text that follows is taken from that Report as published by the government of the DRV:

It is the unswerving policy of the Government of the Democratic Republic of Vietnam to strictly respect the 1954 Geneva Agreements on Vietnam, and to correctly implement their basic provisions as embodied in the following points:

1. Recognition of the basic national rights of the Vietnamese people: peace, independence, sovereignty, unity and territorial integrity. According to the Geneva Agreements, the U.S. Government must withdraw from South Vietnam all U.S. troops, military personnel and weapons of all kinds, dismantle all U.S. military bases there, cancel its "military alliance" with South Vietnam. It must end its policy of intervention and aggression in South Vietnam. According to the Geneva Agreements, the U.S. Government must stop its acts of war against North Vietnam, end definitely all encroachments on the territory and sovereignty of the Democratic Republic of Vietnam.

2. Pending the peaceful reunification of Vietnam, while Vietnam is still temporarily divided into two zones the military provisions of the 1954 Geneva Agreements on Vietnam must be strictly respected: the two zones must refrain from joining any military alliance with foreign countries, there must be no foreign military bases, troops, and military personnel in their respective territory.

3. The affairs of South Vietnam must be settled by the South Vietnamese people themselves, in accordance with the program of the South Vietnam National Liberation Front, without any foreign interference.

4. The peaceful reunification of Vietnam is to be settled by the Vietnamese people in both zones, without any foreign interference.

This stand will certainly enjoy the approval and support of all peace and justice-loving governments and peoples in the world.

The Government of the Democratic Republic of Vietnam is of the view that the above-expounded stand is the basis for the soundest political settlement of the Vietnam question. If this basis is recognized, favorable conditions will be created for the peaceful settlement of the Vietnam question and it will be possible to consider the reconvening of an international conference along the pattern of the 1954 Geneva Conference on Vietnam.

The Government of the Democratic Republic of Vietnam declares that any approach contrary to the above stand is inappropriate; any approach tending to secure a U.N. intervention in the Vietnam affair is also inappropriate because such approaches are basically at variance with the 1954 Geneva Agreements on Vietnam.

V.

SPEECH BY PRIME MINISTER PHAM VAN DONG AT RECEPTION TO SOVIET DELEGATION

In the evening of January 8, 1966, a reception was given by the Central Committee of the Workers Party of Vietnam, for the delegation from the Soviet Union, headed by A. N. Shelepin, member of the Presidium and Secretary of the Central Committee of the Communist Party of the Soviet Union. On that occasion, Premier Pham Van Dong made the speech that is printed below, in full:

Esteemed President Ho Chi Minh,
Dear Comrade Shelepin,
Dear Comrades, Members of the Soviet Delegation,
Dear Comrades and Friends,

On behalf of the Central Committee of the Party of Working People, the Government of the Democratic Republic of Vietnam and the whole Vietnamese people, I warmly greet the Soviet delegation led by Comrade Shelepin. This visit is of tremendous significance. It is evidence of sympathy and support from the fraternal Soviet people, the Communist Party and the government of the Soviet Union, of their great assistance to the Vietnamese people, who are now on the frontline of the struggle against the U. S. imperialist aggressor.

The Vietnamese people have always looked with love and gratitude on the Soviet people, who accomplished the Great October Revolution, established the world's first state of workers and peasants, saved mankind from enslavement by German-Italian-Japanese fascism, created favorable conditions for the success of the revolution in many European and Asian countries, and who invariably supported and helped the cause of the revolution in Vietnam.

Over almost half a century the Soviet people, led by the CPSU, the party of the great Lenin, held its own against severe trials and transformed what had been the backward Russia of the tsars into a great socialist power. Today the Soviet people are bending all their efforts to lay the material and technical foundations for communism.

The Vietnamese people are happy about the impressive achievements of the Soviet people and wholeheartedly wish them still greater progress in building up the material and technical base for communism and in fighting for world peace.

The current developments in Vietnam have seriously alarmed the peoples of the world. The U. S. imperialists are contemplating new, highly dangerous steps in their war of aggression against our country.

After sending an expeditionary corps about 200,000 strong to South Vietnam, the U. S. imperialists vainly hoped for a reversal in the trend of events. They talked a great deal about a "miraculous turn in the war" and claimed that they had succeeded in "checking the surge" of the patriotic war in South Vietnam. In reality, however, the U. S. expeditionary corps has been dealt a series of surprise blows that hit it in both the dry and the rainy season, in the plains, the mountains, in the very center of Saigon and in many other cities. The tide of the people's war has never stopped and, indeed, has gone on rising. The U. S. expeditionary troops have proved to be poor fighters and large units of these troops have been routed. The "miraculous turn in the war," when it comes, will mean only this, that the 200,000-strong expeditionary force will be crushed even if its strength is increased to 300,000, 400,000 or even more.

Far from daunting the Vietnamese people, the destructive air war the U. S. imperialists are waging in the North has made the population of the North hate the U. S. aggressor more than ever and has prompted them to redouble ther efforts on the home and war fronts. It has prompted the people of Vietnam to rally closer together and to inflict heavier losses on the U. S. imperialists. The more the Americans step up and expand the war, the more resounding will their defeat be. The Vietnamese people will win.

Vietnamese history, especially since the establishment of the DRV, shows that our people have always longed to live a free and peaceful life. To achieve this great goal, we have had to fight steadfastly to defeat the imperialist aggressors and regain national independence and peace. The U. S. imperialists' aggressive policy was the chief cause of the war in Vietnam and actually triggered it. Peace in Vietnam will be restored as soon as the U. S. imperialists stop their aggression.

Of late the U. S. government has been carrying on a fraudulent "peace" campaign, making out its "bombing pause" to be a sign of goodwill. President Johnson declared that the United States would keep up its effort for peace, and advanced so-called new peace proposals.

But do the Americans' deeds square with their professed desire for peace?

Not at all. The U. S. rulers persist in their policy of aggression in Vietnam and hang on to South Vietnam, in an attempt to perpetuate the division of our country. This is perfectly clear from Johnson's 14 points and the Americans' recent pronouncements. They show why the U. S. rulers reject the DRV's four-point proposals, especially the very important Point 3, which is inseparable from the other points. They show why the Americans refuse to recognize the National Liberation Front of South Vietnam. True, they speak of the 1954 Geneva Agreements, but what they read into them is intended to perpetuate the division of our country.

Moreover, American "peace" speeches are followed by moves escalating the war. The United States is pouring more troops into South Vietnam and conducting large-scale punitive operations, using strategic aircraft to bomb densely populated areas and destroying numerous villages. More and more it is using chemicals and poison gas for the massive destruction of civilians and crops. Not long ago a large group of American generals arrived in Saigon to discuss measures for expanding "aid" to the puppets and the war of aggression. In North Vietnam, U. S. aircraft daily carry out training flights along the coast and reconnaissance flights in preparation for new raids. In addition, the U. S. imperialists are stepping up air raids on the liberated regions of Laos and brazenly discuss plans for invading Central and South Laos and Cambodia.

What is the meaning of the U. S. rulers' "peace offensive"?

With regard to the American and other peoples, they need a smoke-screen to somehow reassure public opinion, which emphatically condemns their aggressive war in Vietnam.

116

With regard to the Vietnamese people, they are out to impose their own terms. In other words, they want to push through their plan for negotiations from strength. Our people will never accept that.

The DRV government considers it necessary to expose before American and world opinion the real nature of the U. S. "peace offensive" and to show that this campaign is merely the prelude to a further, exceedingly dangerous criminal escalation, to an intensification of the aggressive war in the South and in the North.

In reply to the U. S. aggressors' fraud, a spokesman for our Foreign Ministry pointed out on January 4:

"A political settlement of the Vietnamese problem can be considered only when the U. S. government accepts the four-point proposal of the government of the Democratic Republic of Vietnam, proves this by concrete deeds and at the same time discontinues, once and for all and unconditionally, the air raids and all other acts of war against the DRV. . . . As long as the U. S. imperialists continue their war of aggression in Vietnam, use U. S. troops and those of their satellites invading South Vietnam, and carry on air raids on the DRV, the people of both zones of Vietnam, undaunted by any sacrifices, will staunchly wage the war of resistance to the finish, will fulfill their sacred duty by upholding the sovereignty and independence of their country and by promoting world peace."

The Central Committee of the National Liberation Front of South Vietnam stressed on January 5: "The population of South Vietnam resolutely condemns the brutal conduct of the U. S. authorities, which are stepping up the war and threatening to escalate it still further. The bombing of the North by the U. S. government is an act of aggression, and it must be stopped once and for all and without any conditions. The U. S. imperialists comport themselves in South Vietnam like pirates breaking into a house to kill and plunder. They must leave South Vietnam, and they have no right to advance any demands unless they want to be completely destroyed.

"The population of South Vietnam and the National Liberation Front fully approve the correct and clear position of the patriots of the North set forth in the four-point statement of the DRV government and in the January 4 statement of the DRV Foreign Ministry regarding the recent 'peace efforts' of the United States. . . . The population of South Vietnam will spare no effort to carry out its sacred duty to the country—to 'liberate the South and protect the North'."

117

While escalating the war in Vietnam, the U. S. imperialists have brazenly engaged in aggressive maneuvers all over Indochina. They are feverishly preparing to step up their military operations in Laos, and are gravely endangering the neutrality of the Kingdom of Cambodia. The Vietnamese people emphatically condemn the U. S. imperialists' policy of intervention and aggression toward the countries of Indochina. They stand firmly by the Laotian people, who uphold the 1962 Geneva Agreements on Laos, and by the Khmer people, who uphold the independence, neutrality and territorial integrity of Cambodia.

The Vietnamese people firmly support the Chinese people's struggle to retrieve Taiwan, and inalienable part of Chinese territory, and vigorously protest against the incursions of U.S. aircraft and warships into the air space and territorial waters of the People's Republic of China.

The Vietnamese people firmly support the struggle of the government and people of the Korean People's Democratic Republic and the struggle of the Japanese people against the so-called Japanese-Korean treaty, that infamous maneuver the U. S. imperialists and their agents are carrying out in line with the U. S. policy of aggression and intervention in Northeast Asia.

The Vietnamese people firmly support the struggle of the Soviet Union and the other East European socialist countries against the U. S. imperialists' scheme to provide West Germany with nuclear weapons, and against West German revenge-seeking militarism, a grave menace to European peace and security.

The Vietnamese people firmly support the struggle of the heroic Cuban people, who are repelling the U. S. imperialists' subversive and aggressive maneuvers as they bear aloft the banner of revolution in Latin America.

The Vietnamese people firmly support the gallant struggle of the oppressed peoples—a struggle bound to end in victory—against imperialism and colonialism headed by the U. S. imperialists, for liberation and a new life. At present these people champion unity, struggle and victory at the tricontinental conference in Havana.

The Vietnamese people's increasingly impressive victories in their just struggle against U. S. aggression, for national salvation, are inseparable from the full approval, support and assistance of the fraternal socialist countries and the forces of progress all over the world.

The Communist Party, the government and the people of the Soviet

Union have expressed sincere approval of our fight against U. S. aggression, for national liberation, and have been giving us much valuable assistance in this fight.

The recent session of the Supreme Soviet of the USSR issued a statement supporting Vietnam and urging the parliaments of all nations to oppose the U. S. war of aggression in Vietnam. The statement denounces the U. S. imperialists and stresses that "the Soviet Union, in fulfilling its internationalist duty, has been rendering all-round support and assistance to the Vietnamese people fighting against the aggression of U. S. imperialism, and will continue to do so. . . . The Supreme Soviet of the Union of Soviet Socialist Republics fully shares the attitude of the government of the Democratic Republic of Vietnam and the National Liberation Front of South Vietnam toward the settlement of the Vietnamese problem." In a message to Chairman Nguyen Huu Tho on the fifth anniversary of the founding of the NLFSV, Comrades Brezhnev, Podgorny and Kosygin stated that "the just struggle of the South Vietnamese patriots against the U. S. aggressor will certainly be crowned with success. The U. S. imperialists are heading for inevitable defeat in South Vietnam."

On December 31, 1965, when the U. S. rulers were carrying on their "peace offensive," Comrade Kosygin made the following statement answering some Japanese newspapers and news agencies:

"The Soviet government and people denounce the U. S. aggression against the Vietnamese people. . . . The Soviet government fully subscribes to and supports the attitude of the DRV and the NLFSV toward the settlement of the Vietnamese problem. The United States should immediately discontinue its acts of aggression against the Democratic Republic of Vietnam. In keeping with the Geneva Agreements, the U. S. government should withdraw its troops and armaments from South Vietnam and discontinue aggression against it. The affairs of South Vietnam should be settled by the South Vietnamese people without foreign interference. The peaceful unification of Vietnam should be accomplished by the Vietnamese people themselves, on the basis of the Geneva Agreements."

The People's Republic of China, a big neighboring country linked with Vietnam by close ties, has always warmly and sincerely approved of the revolutionary cause of our people and given them important help in the struggle against U. S. aggression, for national salvation.

The other fraternal parties, acting in the spirit of proletarian internationalism, have also wholeheartedly approved and supported the just struggle of our people.

Today, welcoming the Soviet delegation on its friendly visit to Vietnam, I wish to voice once again the deep gratitude of the Vietnamese people for the important and valuable assistance being given by the people, the Communist Party and the government of the Soviet Union, and also by China and other fraternal socialist countries.

The Vietnamese people are determined to do all in their power to cement fraternal friendship with the Soviet people.

The Vietnamese people are also determined to do their utmost to promote the unity of the socialist camp and the world working-class movement on the basis of Marxism-Leninism and proletarian internationalism.

The Vietnamese people feel certain that thanks to their unity and struggle and to the sympathy, support and assistance of the fraternal socialist countries, the working class of the world and progressive mankind, they will defeat U. S. imperialism, successfully defend the North, liberate the South, and advance to the peaceful reunification of their country, thereby furthering peace in Indochina, Southeast Asia and the rest of the world.

Dear comrades, I propose a toast:

— To the success of the friendly visit of the Soviet delegation to Vietnam.

— To still greater achievements of the fraternal Soviet people in laying the material and technical foundations for communism and in fighting for world peace.

— To everlasting friendship between Vietnam and the Soviet Union.

— To the unity of the socialist camp and of the world Communist movement on the basis of Marxism-Leninism and proletarian internationalism.

— To world peace and friendship among nations.

— To the health of Comrade Brezhnev, Comrade Kosygin, Comrade Podgorny and the other Soviet Party leaders and statesmen.

— To the health of President Ho Chi Minh.

— To the health of Comrade Shelepin and the other members of the Soviet delegation.

To the health of all those present here.

120

VI.

TO THE EVANGELICAL CHRISTIANS AND MINISTERS OF ALL CREEDS IN THE USA*

Hanoi, December 23, 1965.

On the occasion of Christmas, the birthday of Jesus Christ, the day symbolizing peace, on behalf of all Catholic and Evangelical Christians and ministers of the Democratic Republic of Vietnam, the National Liaison Committee of Vietnamese Catholics and the Vietnam General and Evangelical Church would like to extend to you the best wishes, the ones sung by angels during the night of Christ's nativity: "Glory to God in the highest, and on earth peace, good will toward men."

We would like to tell you something that comes from the depth of our hearts.

Dear friends, Christmas means Peace, Happiness and Home. But due to U.S. intervention and aggression, Vietnam, our country, has remained partitioned throughout the past ten years and more.

All during these years, in the South of our country, the U.S. and its puppets have arrested, tortured and thrown into prison great numbers of innocent people. They have used napalm and phosphorus bombs and toxic chemicals to massacre our compatriots. They have bombed and strafed and razed to the ground whole villages, killing many clergymen and believers, and destroying many places of worship of various religions.

As regards the North of our country, since February this year, the U.S. government have been sending aircraft for daily raids against villages, towns, schools, hospitals, irrigational works, and even against churches—the sanctuary of Christ—destroying holy objects, killing Christians and Ministers right in their devout acts. Over fifty churches have been destroyed in the North of our country so far.

The U.S. ruling circles have perpetrated indescribable crimes against the Vietnamese people. Yet, U.S. President Lyndon Johnson of late

* This appeal was given me in Hanoi by church authorities, with the request that I see to its publication in the United States. It was sent by this author to *Commonweal,* the leading lay Catholic magazine, and to *The Christian Century,* leading lay Protestant weekly; neither, however, published it.

121

has decided to increase to 350,000 or 400,000 the present 200,000-strong U.S. army in South Vietnam, and threatened to bomb the most populated towns and cities of North Vietnam such as Haiphong and Hanoi. On the other hand, he is tirelessly swearing that he only wishes "peace" and "negotiation," and tirelessly evokes the Name of Christ in his speeches. This was indeed an offense against the Holy Name and a hypocritical statement of Pharisees.

Our people ardently cherish peace, but this must be peace as advocated by Jesus Christ, peace in freedom, independence, justice and fraternity, not the kind of peace under domination by the aggressors and their lackeys.

We are ready to make all sacrifices to achieve this genuine peace, and we are convinced that we shall be successful for we are acting in accordance with the will of Christ.

Dear friends,

The aggression committed by the U.S. imperialists in Vietnam has caused untold suffering to our people. Likewise, it has also claimed the lives of the husbands and sons of so many families in the United States and caused constant anxiety to many other families about the lives of their beloved ones. Tens of thousands of honest American youth have been turned into murderers in service of the selfish interests of a gang of warmongers and a great number of them die a violet death during raids to massacre innocent people.

That is precisely why more and more American people of all strata, including members of various religious communities and organizations, clergymen and the faithful, have valiantly raised their voice and taken part in demonstrations to protest against the barbarous aggressive policy of the Johnson government and demand an end to the U.S. unjust and completely futile war in Vietnam.

These struggles have greatly encouraged our people.

We take this opportunity to express our sincere thanks to the American people, clergymen and co-religionists. At the same time, we earnestly call on all of you to continue, together with the American and world people, to expose the deceitful tricks and the war intensification and expansion schemes of the Johnson government. Let us demand that the Johnson government stop at once its unjust and barbarous war which runs counter to Christ's will and man's aspirations, and that it halt its bombing of the Democratic Republic of Vietnam, withdraw forthwith troops and weapons of the U.S. and its

122

satellites from South Vietnam and let the Vietnamese people settle by themselves their own affairs just as Christ had said: "Render unto Caesar the things which are Caesar's."

That is the only correct way to bring about peace in Vietnam and contribute to defending world peace.

That is the only way conforming to Christ's teachings. May God bless all of you and the entire American people.

<table>
<tr><td>On behalf of the National
Liaison Committee of
Vietnamese Catholics
    Vice-president,
s/ REV. HO-THANH-BIEN</td><td>On behalf of the
Vietnamese Evangelical
Church
    General Secretary,
s/ REV. BUI-HOANH-THU</td></tr>
</table>

VII.

PRIME MINISTER PHAM VAN DONG'S ANSWERS TO QUESTIONS PUT BY THREE AMERICAN PEACE FIGHTERS

(January 8, 1966)

Question 1: What is your comment on the idea that the Democratic Republic of Vietnam and National Liberation Front refuse all offers to negotiate? Is it not the case that the Democratic Republic of Vietnam and the NLF set conditions for negotiations? What must the United States do before there can be negotiations?

Answer: I am not going to answer in the place of the South Vietnam National Liberation Front.

As far as the Government of the Democratic Republic of Vietnam is concerned, may I quote a few sentences from the January 4, 1966, Statement of our Foreign Ministry. These sentences are:

"It is the unswerving stand of the Government of the Democratic Republic of Vietnam to strictly respect the 1954 Geneva Agreements on Vietnam, and to correctly implement their basic provisions as concretely expressed in the following points: (i.e. the four-point stand of the Government of the Democratic Republic of Vietnam, made public on April 8, 1965. *See* Document IV).

"A political settlement of the Vietnam problem can be envisaged only when the U.S. Government has accepted the four-point stand of the Government of the Democratic Republic of Vietnam, has proved this by actual deeds, at the same time has stopped unconditionally and for good its air raids and all other acts of war against the Democratic Republic of Vietnam."

Question 2: What is the meaning of the third point of Premier Pham Van Dong, "the internal affairs of South Vietnam must be settled by the South Vietnamese people themselves, in accordance with the program of the NLF"?

Answer: The third point is a very important one in the four-point stand of the Government of the Democratic Republic of Vietnam from which it can by no means be dissociated. The U.S. authorities have recently stated that they do not accept this point. Thus they recognize neither the sacred right to self-determination of the people of South Vietnam, nor the National Liberation Front, the sole genuine representative of the people of South Vietnam. In short, they do not accept the four-point stand of the Government of the Democratic Republic of Vietnam, which means they are still pursuing a policy of aggression in South Vietnam.

Question 3: If the United States withdrew its troops, would the DRV withdraw its troops from South Vietnam?

Answer: The so-called "presence of forces of the Democratic Republic of Vietnam in South Vietnam" is a sheer U.S. fabrication in order to justify their war of aggression in South Vietnam.

Question 4: Exactly how would the creation of a national coalition government in South Vietnam and the eventual reunification of South with North Vietnam come about?

Answer: The setting up of a national coalition government in South Vietnam is an internal affair of the people of South Vietnam. It is to be settled by the people of South Vietnam themselves in accordance with the program of the National Liberation Front. This program provides for the establishment of "a broad national democratic coalition government including representatives of all strata of the people, of all nationalities, political parties, and religious communities, and of patriotic personalities. We must wrest back the people's economic, political, social and cultural rights, realize independence and democracy, improve the people's living conditions, carry out a policy of peace and neutrality and advance toward peaceful reunification of the Fatherland."

124

The reunification of Vietnam is an internal affair of the Vietnamese people, it is to be settled by the Vietnamese people in the two zones. On this subject, it is said in the program of the South Vietnam National Liberation Front:

"The urgent demand of our people throughout the country is to reunify the Fatherland by peaceful means. The South Vietnam National Liberation Front advocates the gradual reunification of the country by peaceful means, through negotiations and discussions between the two zones on all forms and measures beneficial to the Vietnamese people and Fatherland."

And the Program of the Vietnam Fatherland Front reads in part:

"To achieve in favorable conditions the peaceful reunification of our Fatherland, we must take into account the real situation in the two zones, the interests and legitimate aspirations of all sections of the population. At the same time, we must conduct negotiations to arrange the holding of free general elections in order to achieve national unity without either side trying to exert pressure on, or trying to annex the other."

Question 5: Would the Geneva Conference be reconvened?

Answer: In reply to this question, I would like to quote a sentence from the April 8, 1965, Statement of the Government of the Democratic Republic of Vietnam about our four-point stand: "If this basis (i.e. the four-point stand) is recognized, favorable conditions will be created for the peaceful settlement of the Vietnam question and it will be possible to consider the reconvening of an international conference along the pattern of the 1954 Geneva Conference on Vietnam."

Question 6: It is often said by the United States government that the NLF is an agent of the Democratic Republic of Vietnam, and that the Democratic Republic of Vietnam is controlled by the Chinese People's Republic. What is your reply?

Answer: This is a vile fabrication designed to slander the Vietnamese people, the South Vietnam National Liberation Front, the Democratic Republic of Vietnam and the People's Republic of China.

The South Vietnam National Liberation Front is the sole genuine representative of the people of South Vietnam, it enjoys great prestige among the people of South Vietnam and in the world, it is now leading the infinitely heroic and certain to be victorious fight waged by the people of South Vietnam against U.S. imperialist aggression. The U.S.

refusal to recognize the South Vietnam National Liberation Front shows all the more clearly that the U.S. Government is bent on pursuing the war of aggression in South Vietnam, consequently, it will sustain even heavier defeats.

The Democratic Republic of Vietnam is a socialist, independent and sovereign country. Its relations with the brotherly People's Republic of China are founded on the principle of total equality, cooperation and mutual aid. These are relations between comrades-in-arms, as close with each other as lips and teeth.

A Selected Bibliography

Aptheker, Herbert: *American Foreign Policy and the Cold War*, N.Y., 1962, New Century, esp. pp. 264-90, 341-60.

—— "Vietnam: Life or Death?" in *Political Affairs*, April, 1965.

—— "Further on Vietnam," in *Political Affairs*, June, 1965.

Bator, Victor: *Vietnam: A Diplomatic Tragedy*, N.Y. 1965, Oceana Pub.

Browne, M. D.: *The New Face of War*, N.Y., 1965, Bobbs-Merrill.

Browne, R. S.: "The Freedom Movement and the War in Vietnam," *Freedomways*, Fall, 1965.

Burchett, Wilfred: *The Furtive War: The United States in Vietnam and Laos*, N.Y., 1963, International Publishers.

—— *Vietnam: Inside Story of the Guerilla War*, N.Y., 1965, International Publishers.

Buttinger, Joseph: *The Smaller Dragon: A Political History of Vietnam*, N.Y., 1958, Praeger.

Carver, G. A. Jr.: "The Real Revolution in South Vietnam," *Foreign Affairs*, April, 1965.

Cary, S. G.: "Three Months in Vietnam," *The Progressive*, Oct. 1965.

Clubb, O. E. Jr.: *The United States and the Sino-Soviet Bloc in Southeast Asia*, Washington, 1962, Brookings Institute.

Cole, A. B. and others, eds., *Conflict in Indochina and International Repercussions: A Documentary History, 1945-1955*, Ithaca, 1956, Cornell Univ. Press.

Colodny, R. G.: "Vietnam: The Politics of Despair," *Nomos* (Pittsburgh), June, 1965.

Deane, Hugh: *War in Vietnam*, N.Y., 1965, Monthly Review Pamphlet.

Devillers, P.: "Struggle for the Unification of Vietnam," *The China Quarterly*, Jan.-March, 1962.

Fall, Bernard B.: *The Two Vietnams: A Political and Military Analysis*, N.Y., 1964, Praeger.

Fifield, R. H.: *The Diplomacy of Southeast Asia, 1945-58*, N.Y., 1958, Harper.

Fishel, W. R., ed.: *Problems of Peace: Vietnam Since Independence*, N.Y., 1961, Free Press.

Fleming, D. F., "Can We Play God in Asia?" *The Progressive*, June, 1965

Gannett, Betty: *End the War in Vietnam!*, N.Y., 1965, New Outlook pamphlet.

Gettleman, Marvin E.: *Vietnam: History, Documents and Opinions*, N.Y., 1965, Fawcett.

Gittings, John: "A Basis for Negotiation Exists," *The Nation*, Sept. 6, 1965.

Halberstam, David: *The Making of a Quagmire*, N.Y., 1964, Random House.

Hall, D. G., ed.: *A History of South-East Asia*, London, 1964, Macmillan.

Hammer, Ellen J.: *The Struggle for Indochina*, Stanford, 1954, Stanford Univ. Press.

Ho Chi Minh, "The Vietnamese Revolution," *New Times* (Moscow), Sept. 8, 1965.

Honey, P. J.; *North Vietnam Today*, N.Y., 1962, Praeger.

Institute of Pacific Relations: *Documents of the 1945 Revolution in Vietnam*, N.Y., 1963.

Kahin, G. M., ed.: *Government and Politics of Southeast Asia*, Ithaca, 1964, Cornell Univ. Press.

Koch, Chris: "An Eyewitness in the North," *Viet-Report*, Oct. 1965.

Lacouture, Jean: *Vietnam: Between Two Truces*, N.Y., 1966, Random House.

Lancaster, Donald: *The Emancipation of French Indo-China*, London, N.Y., 1961, Oxford Univ. Press.

Larson, D. R. and Larson, Arthur: *Vietnam and Beyond: A New American Foreign Policy and Program*, Durham, 1965, Duke Univ. Press, pamphlet.

Lawyers Committee on American Policy towards Vietnam: *American Policy vis-a-vis Vietnam: Memorandum of Law,* N.Y., 1965, printed in *Congressional Record,* Sept. 23, 1965.

McDermott, John, "The History of Vietnam," three-part article in *Viet-Report,* June-Nov., 1965.

Mecklin, John: *Mission in Torment: An Intimate Account of the U.S. Role in Vietnam,* N.Y., 1965, Doubleday.

Morgenthau, H. J., *Vietnam and the United States,* Washington, 1965, Public Affairs Press.

Myerson, Michael, *United States and Vietnam,* San Francisco, 1965, Du Bois Club pamphlet.

—— "Eyewitness in North Vietnam," *Insurgent,* Nov.-Dec. 1965.

Perlo, V. and Goshal, Kumar: *Bitter End in Southeast Asia,* N.Y., 1964, Marzani & Munsell.

Ramparts, the issues of July, 1965 and February, 1966 are devoted largely to Vietnam.

Raskin, M. G. and Fall, B., eds., *Vietnam Reader,* N.Y. 1965, Random House.

Roy, Jules: *The Battle of Dienbienphu,* N.Y., 1965, Harper & Row.

Scheer, Robert: *How the United States Got Involved in Vietnam,* Santa Barbara, 1965, Center for Study of Democratic Institutions, pamphlet.

Schopmer, Howard: *Runaway War or Deadlocked Peace,* Chicago, 1965, Christian Century pamphlet.

Shaplen, Robert: *The Lost Revolution,* N.Y., 1965, Harper & Row.

Stone, I. F.: "Vietnam: An Exercise in Self-Delusion," *N.Y. Review of Books,* April 22, 1965.

Tanham, G. K.: *Communist Revolutionary Warfare: The Vietminh in Indochina,* N.Y., 1961, Praeger.

See also, *The Conscience of the Senate,* a pamphlet published by Marzani & Munsell, N.Y., 1965, containing anti-war speeches made in the Senate; and the entire file of the magazine *Viet-Report,* including reports made by Staughton Lynd and Tom Hayden upon their return from our journey.

128